The Virtual Reference Handbook

INTERVIEW AND INFORMATION DELIVERY TECHNIQUES FOR THE CHAT AND E-MAIL ENVIRONMENTS

Diane K. Kovacs

Neal-Schuman Publishers, Inc.

New York   London

Don't miss the companion Web site that accompanies this book available at: www.kovacs.com/ns/chatrefbook/chatrefbook.html

Login name: NealSchuman
Password: kovacs

Published by Neal-Schuman Publishers, Inc.
100 William Street, Suite 2004
New York, NY 10038–4512

Copyright © 2007 Neal-Schuman Publishers, Inc.

Printed and bound in the United States of America.

The paper used in this publication meets the minimum requirements of American National Standard for Information Sciences – Permanence of Paper for Printed Library Materials, ANSI Z39.48–1992.

ISBN–13: 978–1-55570–598-5
ISBN-10: 1-55570-598-7

Library of Congress Cataloging-in-Publication Data

Kovacs, Diane K. (Diane Kaye), 1962–
    The virtual reference handbook : interview and information delivery techniques for the chat and e-mail environments / Diane K. Kovacs.
        p. cm.
    Includes bibliographical references and index.
    ISBN 1-55570-598-7 (alk. paper)
    1. Electronic reference services (Libraries) I. Title.
Z711.45V574 2007
025.5'2—dc22
                                                                    2006035099

Contents

Chapter 3: Practice and Expand Communications Skills and Knowledge for the Virtual Reference Interview   59

Preface

The Web-based workshops and courses I teach sometimes feature a live online chat component where we participate in real-time class discussions. Students type their comments and ask questions. I post my lecture, lead discussions, and answer questions. Everyone can contribute and follow along in the main classroom chat window. One of the librarians, experiencing her first online chat encounter, asked me a vital question: "How can librarians learn all these technical and communications skills, resources, delivery mechanisms, and all the other stuff that we need to know to be a virtual reference librarian?" Her question made me think carefully about what it takes to be a competent virtual reference librarian today. What is it exactly that we need to learn? Why do we need to learn it? Where can we turn for information and assistance?

I certainly know why people should seek our services. Librarians have reference expertise—the knowledge and skill to:

- search sources,
- think critically,
- analyze questions,
- interview,
- organize information,
- locate specific reference sources, and
- master advanced information-finding tools.

It is these skills that will attract Web searchers to professional virtual reference services, rather than just using Google and hoping for the best.

I designed *The Virtual Reference Handbook* for librarians, library school students, and library paraprofessionals who want to:

- acquire and improve their technical skills,
- maintain and build on their repertoire of reference skills and knowledge, and
- practice and expand their chat and e-mail reference communication skills in particular.

The handbook balances practical learning activities with up-to-date information, sensible advice, and shared experiences. It also explores the issue of how to carve out the time to learn or review and reinforce your skills. Finally, it includes transcripts of e-mail conversations with eight virtual reference librarians on various topics, selected to illustrate, clarify, or provide alternative points of view.

The Virtual Reference Handbook is designed to work equally well for individual self-paced learning or group instruction. All learning activities, readings, and core resources lists are available through a supplemental Web site to facilitate their use and to keep them current. To log in, connect to www.kovacs.com/ns/chatrefbook/chatrefbook.html.

Handbook Structure

The chapters explore four different areas; each one offers hands-on learning activities, features tips from accomplished reference librarians, and includes recommended reading lists.

Chapter 1, "Technical, Communications, and Reference Skills and Knowledge for Virtual Reference Librarians," explores the foundations and fundamentals of this service and its most critical aspect: the reference interview. It examines all the technical skills and indispensable communications knowledge necessary to greet this challenge competently, whether face-to-face, on the phone, through chat, or via e-mail. This chapter also introduces virtual reference competencies—the basic and advanced skills and knowledge needed to perform chat and e-mail reference fluently.

Experienced reference librarians have expertise in interviewing patrons and utilizing core reference sources. They intuitively understand that the answer is always, "We can try to find the answer," and they know how to begin searching. New reference service providers may need to observe, read about, and practice those skills and knowledge. Everyone begins from a slightly different foundation of skills and knowledge, so a virtual reference competencies self-assessment activity is provided in Chapter 1, to help each librarian establish awareness of the skills and knowledge he or she brings to the learning process.

Chapter 2, "Acquire and Improve Technical Skills and Knowledge for Virtual Reference," describes both basic and advanced technical competencies as well as strategies to acquire and improve them. Tips from conversations with virtual reference librarians and learning activities support skill review and reinforcement.

Chapter 3, "Practice and Expand Communications Skills and Knowledge for the Virtual Reference Interview," advances the basics of the first chapter and discusses ways to practice and expand proficiencies.

Chapter 4, "Maintain and Build Reference Skills and Knowledge," addresses areas both essential and advanced. It suggests ways to maintain and build reference sources and explores patron delivery systems based on service policies for resource access, copyright and/or licensing arrangements—both print and Web-based. It also includes representative core resource and tool lists, because electronic reference collection of both free and fee-based Web-accessible resources is an essential adjunct to good service.

The current *Occupational Outlook Handbook* (available at www.bls.gov/oco/ ocos068.htm) states:

> . . . librarians, or information professionals, increasingly are combining traditional duties with tasks involving quickly changing technology. Librarians assist people in finding information and using it effectively for personal and professional purposes. Librarians must have knowledge of a wide variety of scholarly and public information sources and must follow trends related to publishing, computers, and the media in order to oversee the selection and organization of library materials.

I hope *The Virtual Reference Handbook* will not only help you greet and meet this exciting challenge but also help you find your own personal and professional best as a cutting-edge practitioner, able to offer your patrons all the advantages of this amazing new world of the electronic information revolution.

References

Kovacs, Diane K., and Kara L. Robinson. 2004. *The Kovacs Guide to Electronic Library Collection Development: Essential Core Subject Collections, Selection Criteria, and Guidelines*. New York: Neal-Schuman.

Definitions and Competencies

... I sometimes worry that virtual reference may be too limiting a vision, too literal a translation of the practices of physical libraries to the networked world, too much of a future glimpsed through a rear-view mirror. "Virtual reference" has a bit of an echo with concepts like "horseless carriage" and may ultimately join the horseless carriage in the catalog of yesterday's tomorrows. I find myself wondering whether it may be more productive to think more broadly about network-based library services and library presence in evolving network-based communities. But it's a place to start, and we often first have to position new developments by analogy to existing technologies and services before we can really understand them in their own right.

—Clifford Lynch, Foreword to *The Virtual Reference Librarian's Handbook,* by Anne Grodzins Lipow

Virtual Reference, Chat, and Instant Messaging

I agree with Cliff Lynch that the term "virtual reference" is something like the term "horseless carriage." The distinction? We provide reference face-to-face and through other means, such as phone, fax, mail, etc. We provide virtual reference service through the Web—using chat with various software platforms, or Instant Messaging. Chat refers to almost real-time text-based communication. Most of it takes place through Web applications referred to collectively as IM or Instant Messaging.

See also http://en.wikipedia.org/wiki/Chat links

Librarians and Users

Users, patrons, clients, or customers are some of the traditional definitions of the people seeking reference services. In this book they are called "computer users" or "service users." The term "librarian" is used for the providers, in solidarity with the American Library Association's 2004 edition of *Guidelines for Behavioral Performance of Reference and Information Service Providers,* which states "The term librarian . . . applies to all who provide reference and informational services directly to library users." (Available at http://www.ala.org/ala/rusa/rusaprotools/referenceguide/htm). Virtual reference librarian refers to all those librarians who provide reference services via the Web, through either chat or e-mail.

Information Delivery

Information delivery—when users receive the information they need, in a form they can use—is the ultimate outcome of reference service.

Referrals to other appropriate information sources or search options depends on the user's affiliations and status under the policies and licensing agreements of the referral library or library organization

Reference and Virtual Reference Librarian Competencies

Competencies refer to the skills required to provide effective reference service. These basic or advanced abilities are organized in *The Virtual Reference Handbook* according to technical, communications, and reference skills and knowledge. The competencies identified for this handbook are synthesized from a review of the library literature and e-mail conversations with virtual reference librarians. Reference librarian competencies, and specifically those competencies required to excel at offering virtual reference services, are frequent topics for research and practical articles in the library and information sciences literature.*

Competency Terminology

The learning goals and performance objectives featured in this handbook utilize the following expressions.

- "Demonstrate awareness of" means the learner knows and can explain to others that a given concept, skill, or activity exists and that the learner can find out more about it.
- "Understanding of" means the learner can write or talk effectively about a given concept, skill, or activity and apply it to appropriate situations. Understanding exceeds mere awareness in that it "is a psychological process related to an abstract or physical object, such as, person, situation and message whereby one is able to think about it and use concepts to deal adequately with that object"—http://en.wikipedia.org/wiki/Understanding—as opposed to just knowing that the concept, skill, or activity exists.
- "Ability to" means that the learner is able to actually perform an activity or identified skill.

- "Detailed functional knowledge" means that the learner is able to actually perform an activity or identified skill, and to teach others; the learner can write or talk in detail about the underlying concept of an identified skill or activity and apply it to appropriate situations

*See the reference lists at the end of each chapter.

Titles especially recommended are:

- Nofsinger, 1999;
- Meola and Stormont, 2002;
- Smith, 2002;
- Ronan, 2003a, Ronan, 2003b;
- Lipow, 2003;
- Hirko and Ross, 2004;
- ALA/RUSA, 2004; DREI, 2004;
- Salem, Balraj and Lilly, 2004;
- Lindbloom, Yackle, Burhans, Peters, and Bell, 2006; and
- Westbrook, 2006.

E-mail Conversations with Virtual Reference Librarians Group

Identifier	Name, Title, E-mail	Organization	Type of Service	Website
KP	Kristen J. Pool, KnowItNow AfterDark Project Coordinator <kristen.pool@nolanet.org>	KnowItNow 24/7	Ohio—Statewide Public—Chat Reference Service	http://www.knowitnow.org/
SM	Sharon Morris, MLS, AskColorado Coordinator, Colorado State Library <sharon.morris@cde.state.co.us>	AskColorado	Colorado—Statewide Public, K–12, Academic, Spanish 24/7—Chat Reference Service	http://www.askcolorado.org/
PO	Penny O'Connor, Assistant Head, Science and Technology Department, Cleveland Public Library, and AfterDark Librarian <penelope.oconnor@cpl.org>	KnowItNow 24/7	Ohio—Statewide Public—Chat Reference Service	http://www.knowitnow.org
JY	Jill Youngs, Business Outreach Librarian <jyoungs@mailbox.lpl.org>	Ask A Librarian	Liverpool Public Library, Liverpool, NY—E-mail Reference Service	http://www.lpl.org
KLR	Kara L. Robinson, Associate Professor, Reference and Instruction Librarian (coordinates Kent State's participation in OhioLINK's chat service) <krobinso@kent.edu>	OhioLINK—Chat with a Librarian	Ohio—Statewide Academic—Chat and E-Mail Reference Service	http://www.ohiolink.edu
LB	Lori Bell, Director of Innovation at Alliance Library System <LBell927@yahoo.com>	AskAwayIllinois Virtual Reference Service	Illinois—Statewide—Chat and E-Mail Reference Service	http://www.askawayillinois.info
JV	Jennifer Varney, Assistant Director <JVarney@blc.org>	Ask24/7	Boston Library Consortium—Academic—Chat Reference Service	http://www.blc.org/247/247Welcome.html or http://www.questionpoint.org/crs/servlet/org.oclc.home.TFSRedirect?VIRTCATEGORY=BOSTON U&SS COMMAND=CUST SUP&Category=BLC
SH	Sonia Araceli Hernández Acuña, Instruction and User Services Librarian <shernand@itesm.mx>	Biblioteca de la Universidad Virtual	Instituto Tecnoló-gico y de Estudios Superiores de Monterrey, Universidad Virtual—México—Chat Reference and Instruction Service	http://bibliotecauv.tecvirtual.com.mx/

Acknowledgments

Michael J. Kovacs should be listed as a co-author. For most of 2006, while I wrote this book, he not only made dinner, but he also acted as my own personal copy editor. His insight as a user of libraries was invaluable.

The concept for this book was born when Stephanie Orphan, e-learning coordinator for ACRL, asked me to develop a WebCast on reference interviewing. While writing this book and considering "what makes a good reference librarian good," I remembered with great fondness the many librarians who made me want to be a librarian when I grew up:

Mrs. Peterson,
Mr. Smith,
Mrs. Ellerby,
Betsy Wilson,
Mary Beth Allen,
Beth Woodard,
Linda Smith,
Leigh Estabrook,
Paul Boytinck (who taught me how to catalog with OCLC),
Kara Robinson,
Leila Balraj,
Jean Smith,
Rosemary Harrick,
Penny O'Connor,
Jean Piety, and most specially,
Anne Lipow (who took the time to talk to me and set my mind on a fruitful path).

Thank you to the virtual reference librarians who patiently allowed me to interview them.

Chapter 1

Technical, Communications, and Reference Skills and Knowledge for Virtual Reference Librarians

> *It's possible to spend thousands of dollars purchasing software and marketing a service, but when it comes to user satisfaction, a virtual reference service such as a real-time chat or e-mail is only as good as the person answering the question at the other end. . . .*
>
> *To meet users' needs rapidly, identify real-time competencies and train staff in these skills. Chat reference competencies include good typing skills, mastery of online information sources, effective interviewing skills, and the ability to solve problems.*
>
> (Ronan, 2003b:79)

What is a reference librarian? Our reason for existence, our purpose, our raison d'etre, is to assist library users—information seekers—in identifying their information needs and locating the desired information within the context of library service.

The library is no longer simply a physical location and collection of physically owned materials, but an entity that encompasses collections of information resources in various formats—print and electronic—that are accessible to the library's users. As our focus shifts from ownership of materials to accessibility of information sources, more and more of our library collection is on the Web. E-library collections as well as physical collections are part of our service to our users. As access to the Web from homes, offices, and schools becomes increasingly ubiquitous, more people are making use of Web-based information services. The challenge is for reference librarians to be there, when and where users need them, on the Web as they have been in the physical library.

Jenny Levine describes this as a need for librarians to shift with current and potential users as their information-seeking behavior changes (Levine, "the Shifted

Librarian" http://www.theshiftedlibrarian.com/stories/2002/01/19/whatIsAShifted
Librarian.html).

Using our e-libraries, Web sites, and related media presence, librarians must
invite users to make use of reference services: to tell librarians about their information needs. Librarians must be there to welcome them, to interview them and to
elicit details needed to help them locate the desired information, and to assist them
in working with the information resources identified together, whether they are
freely available on the Web, in a licensed database that only "officially identified"
library users can access, or in a print or other locally owned format in a physical
library.

This does not mean that reference service in the physical library is replaced by
reference service through the Web. Just as librarians did not stop using print reference tools or reading printed books when some resources became available in electronic formats, they will continue to be needed in physical locations. Librarians
can work well and willingly with both the users that wish to be and can be served
through virtual reference and those that want or need to come to the physical
library.

Users need to be able to identify library reference services as reliable, high-
quality alternatives to just Googling (or using MSNSearch, or Yahoo, etc.). Librarians need to distinguish their services and clarify what it is that they do that is of
service to users. Why should users consult us either in the physical library or on the
Web, instead of just searching themselves? Why is reference service valuable in the
context of the technological environment that has greatly expanded the scope of
user self-service options?

Reference service is distinguished from user self-service by the expectation that
reference librarians know where information is located or may be accessed: how to
find it, how to search it, and how to teach the user to search it. Reference librarians
must also know whether or not information is available for delivery to the user in
the format the user wants or needs, and for a cost—including time, money, and
effort—that the user can afford. Librarians must be superior Web searchers, knowing very well what information can be found and where, and how beyond simple
Web searching of public Web sites. They must be able to analyze the user's question effectively—as an information need—within the context of existing and available information sources, formats, and access modes.

In order to apply the best reference strategies in virtual communications modes,
librarians need to have a firm grounding in interviewing basics, integrated with
knowledge of the structure and availability of information, to use in answering
reference questions and assisting with research needs. Thus, foundations remain
strong as the locus of library reference service shifts from face-to-face to virtual
reference.

The reference interview is an essential aspect of high-quality reference service, whether offered face-to-face or virtually, via chat or e-mail.

In *Conducting the Reference Interview: A How-To-Do-It Manual for Librarians* (2002), Ross, Nilsen, and Dewdney thoroughly cover the most important research and the communications skills and knowledge needed for conducting good reference interviews. Their extensive research and experience leads to their conclusion that, "The principles for the reference interview remain the same, no matter what the environment." (Ross, Nilsen, and Dewdney, 2002:211) Or as Meola and Stormont (2002) put it more poetically: "Think of live virtual reference like vintage wine in a brand new bottle—providing human help to library users is the vintage wine, the Internet is the new bottle . . . " (Meola and Stormont, 2002:3–4)

What is a "Reference Interview"?

At its most basic, a reference interview is a user asking a question and a library staff person helping them to frame their question within the context of information organization, so that it can be answered from existing information sources. Ideally it is a communication interaction between a librarian, designated and trained to provide reference service, and a library user.

The phrase "reference interview" is library jargon used when librarians talk about the process amongst themselves. Library users do not say, "I am going to have a reference interview with the librarian." They will just find a library staff person and ask a question. They may not even know that they can or should ask a librarian. The librarian's job is to anticipate, invite, encourage, accept, and respond to those questions as reference librarians.

The reference interview begins before the user and the question are present. It begins with offering reference services in such a way that users are made aware of them, and in the preparation of highly skilled reference librarians to provide those services.

A reference interview is conducted to elicit the information the user really needs, and the level (educational, reading, etc.); depth (quick answer, research, directional, holdings, policies, etc.); and format (single fact, media, bibliographic, full-text, encyclopedic, books, articles, print, or electronic format) for delivery of the information the user requires. A good reference interview should result in the user receiving the needed information, instructions for accessing the needed information, or an alternative option for acquiring the needed information.

A reference interview is an attempt to find out what the user's question "really" is and to elicit the information the librarian needs in order to answer the user's question accurately. Hirko and Ross (2004:78) call this "getting the question straight."

Reference interviews are the best strategy for finding out what questions library users are really asking and to ensure that the reference interaction is successful. That is, as a result of successful reference interviews, users get the information they need at the level, and depth, they need it and in the format they need and can use.

> A well-conducted reference interview usually is a very short exchange. The librarian may start with an acknowledgment ("Health Information, un-huh") followed by one or two strategic open questions ("What particular aspect of health information are you interested in?" or "What would you like to find out?"). And of course a lot of hard listening.
>
> (Ross, 2003: 38)

Some librarians argue that they don't have time for reference interviews, or that reference interviews are not needed for every reference question. However, ongoing research studies on reference services continue to demonstrate that a reference interview is critical to user satisfaction, as measured by:

- continued use of the reference service by a given user,
- the likelihood that the user will receive a "correct" answer, and
- the expressed willingness of the user to use the library reference service in the future.

A reference interview ultimately saves both the librarian and the user time that would otherwise be wasted in users getting inadequate or unusable information, and drive many of those users to less professionally skilled and knowledgeable sources of assistance for their future information needs. (Nofsinger, 1999; Ross, Nilsen, and Dewdney, 2002; Ross, 2003; Ward, 2003; Nilsen, 2005; Buckley, 2006; Lindbloom, Yackle, Burhans, Peters, and Bell, 2006; Westbrook, 2006)

Successful and positive reference interviews integrate good communications skills and good reference source knowledge

The library user may be asking any one or a combination of the identifiable types of reference questions: known item (holdings), directional/policies and procedures, ready-reference (short answer), specific-search, or research. Good knowledge of the local print and electronic collection, shared Web-accessible fee-based databases, as well as what might be freely available on the Web, along with a thoughtful reference interview, generally suffice for most reference questions. Ideally, the reference librarian's communications skills and reference source knowledge interact to result in a successful and positive outcome of the reference interview. Successful reference interviews conclude with the provision of appropriate information or access instructions for information sources to library users in a format they can use. That is, the reference interview includes the delivery of the information needed or appropriate alternatives.

Positive reference interviews also result in the library user "feeling good" about the communications interaction and anticipating a return to the library for additional virtual or face-to-face reference services.

The next section addresses some commonalities in the reference interview process.

Interview Question I

The librarian, in a good face-to-face, chat, or e-mail reference interview

- uses open-ended questions ("Can you tell me more about what you need to know?" "Is this related to your subject?");
- listens and remembers what the patron says;
- paraphrases what the patron asks, giving the patron the opportunity to correct/expand in his or her own words;
- makes no assumptions about the patron's social or intellectual status;
- repeats the interview strategies detailed above to gather information that will help decide what level of information (e.g., reading level, grade level, etc) and in what subject area the patron needs the information; and
- verifies /follows up with the patron with more open-ended questions ("Is the information provided what you need?" "Do you need more information?").

For the librarian, I find listening and remembering is easier in chat and e-mail because communication is onscreen and can be reread. It is harder to follow up with these patrons because they may not pay attention to the chat if they have gone off to look at the information already provided.

For the patron, it is easier because directions are given in writing rather than in words that they must remember after leaving the librarian.

In your experience, how does the chat/e-mail reference mode make the reference interview more difficult? How does it make it simpler?

KP: The biggest problem I've seen with the online reference interview is that many librarians rely on suggested or prescribed messages that are really ineffective. For instance, we have one that says, "I don't understand your question. Can you be more specific?" Invariably, patrons just retype their original question. In one transcript I read, the patron revised his question "I need information about the Tribes of Israel" to "I need LOTS of information about the Tribes of Israel" when he was sent that question. Another over-used prescribed message is, "Have you done any searching already? If so, where have you looked?" This usually either elicits a grumpy, "Nowhere, I'm asking you," or a disconnect because the patron figures the librarian is reluctant to help him or her.

So what I do and what I stress in training is to, number 1, let the patron know that you are willing to help by sending a message like, "I'm sure we can find something—I just need some clarification first." Then the actual reference interview questions should be in a "multiple choice" sort of format. "Are you looking for statistics for the whole world, or just the United States?" "Do you mean ocean fish, freshwater fish, or aquarium fish?" That is especially effective for patrons who don't type well, rather than asking them an open-ended question that might require a lot of typing.

Also, if I'm working with a patron who is having a very difficult time communicating, either because he or she can't type well, can't express him or herself well, or is very impatient, I'll often send a resource to the patron and *then* do the reference interview—"Is this what you're looking for?" "This is a good overview—is it detailed enough?"

SM: The reference interview is important in an online environment and the following distinguish it from the in-person reference transaction:

- If the customer has the assumption of an online instant answer, they may become impatient with the reference interview.
- Younger patrons, who are instructed not to talk to strangers in an online environment, may find the questions invasive and the librarian rude.
- Younger patrons may find it hard to articulate their information needs. Some prefer you send them something, and then they can comment on whether it is helpful or what more specifically they need. At times, sending resources becomes a part of narrowing down the reference need.

The technique of restating the question seems less awkward online and often functions as a quick way for the librarian to elicit more specific feedback from the patron.

Having the text of the question can be a plus if you don't know how to spell the topic of interest and the customer does. It can delay the reference process if the customer has misspelled words and the librarian needs to clarify the research need.

The librarian has a bit of time to research while conducting the reference interview in the online environment. While waiting for replies from the patron, the librarian can start researching and refining the interview process without appearing to be rude.

PO: Yes to all of the above. Just like with an in-person interview, though, the chat session cannot always provide the complete solution, so we try to complete by e-mail or by suggesting that the patron follow up in the library. It is much easier for the patron to see what we mean, or to provide in-depth information, by pushing a site, or by sending an e-mail that can be used to revisit the links.

Of course, the online medium does often make patrons think that the answer will be instantaneous, just because it is supplied via computer. They don't always grasp that research or even reference does sometimes take time. It is important for the librarian to communicate that he/she is working on the question, to let the patron know that the librarian may be working with others at the same time, and to offer to get back on a lengthy question.

It is not always easy to find something for the patron at their *exact* level, especially when they are in a hurry.

JY: With e-mail reference, not only can the librarian reread the question, but the patron can also reread and refer to the printed response later. I try to answer e-mail reference questions as completely as possible, sometimes "overanswering" a question just to make sure all bases are covered. Chances are that the person who e-mailed the question has gone on to other tasks and will check later for the answer, resulting in a limited opportunity for the give-and-take of a reference interview. If there is a follow-up question or more detail is needed, it might be hours later when another librarian is on duty. We keep our responses with the original question in the OUT mailbox and delete messages in the IN box after they are answered. A continuous log is created by the OUT messages, and if there is a follow-up question, it is most efficient to look at the previous correspondence and formulate a follow-up response from that.

KLR: The patron has to be clearer about what he or she wants in one sense—there is less chance for a communication difficulty because the transaction is written. However, if the patron isn't able to articulate what he or she needs clearly, it is much more difficult to figure it out in writing—you lack visual clues that demonstrate their possible confusion and also the ability to show that you are listening and are concerned about finding them what they need.

In most cases, follow-up is nonexistent in chat. Once that student has what he or she needs, they log off and boom—that's that (of course, if it were IM-based chat, they'd still be in your buddy list and vice versa). In those rare instances where there is follow-up, it is typically the student who still hasn't found what they need coming back to see what else we can suggest.

LB: I think some nonverbal can be emulated but nothing is as good as face-to-face. For a personal question though, the patron might feel safer in the online environment. I tell people not to use all caps as that is yelling. I try to use smiley faces when appropriate, especially with teens. I try to keep in contact during the search to tell people what I am doing. I try not to have typos but sometimes you can't avoid those.

JV: I think they can come pretty close to emulating nonverbal communications. Chat is never going to be the same as a face-to-face conversation. But more and more people, especially younger people, are increasingly comfortable with chat-type communications and can express amazing amounts of information with it. Emoticons, tone, level of formality, attention (or deliberate lack thereof) to grammar and spelling can all contribute to the nonverbal feel of a chat communication. I encourage staff to use emoticons and other clues to achieve approachability. In general I think we mostly try to follow the patron's lead on this one.

SH: The librarian uses open-ended questions—e.g. asking the patron "can you tell me more about what you need to know" or "is this related to X subject?"

Yes, I consider is very appropriate to use them this way. But I will recommend to include guidance along with the question so the user follows our "train of thinking."

*   *The librarian is listening and remembering what the patron says.*

Actually in virtual reference the following can happen:

- When using chat, it can be "forgivable" if the librarian does not "catch" everything because the nature of the chat. (In our system it is possible assist from 1 to 10 users at the same time).
- When using e-mail, it could happen that the librarians do not read all the information or confuse one question previously made with a new one if the writing is similar, so I consider it is extremely important to read carefully each e-mail because not doing it could be compared to "not listening" to a patron.

About "remembering" patron's questions or information, at least that aspect is not a problem in our system, because the software keeps a record of the information that is exchanged during the communication. But if I wasn't working with our system, I would probably save every communication in a separate record, organizing it in a way that can be useful to be recalled.

The librarian is paraphrasing what the patron is asking to give them the opportunity to correct/expand in their own words

This answer is similar to my recommendation on the first question on this section. I believe that it have to be done since the first answer we are replaying, in order to avoid the length of the e-mail exchanging.

The librarian is not making assumptions about the patron's social or intellectual status, but is gathering information that will help decide what level of information (e.g., reading level, grade level, etc) and in what subject area the patron is needing the information by repeating the interview strategies detailed above.

In this case, using distance reference services, I consider it OK to make assumptions to gather information. Because my experience is limited to specific kinds of patrons (university students and teachers in master or doctoral degrees) there is no much room left to make assumptions and the area is clearly defined when the patrons identify themselves but! When I am talking about making assumptions, these are about the purpose of the research that can vary from a simple homework to a thesis or a field project and my answer will differ in depth based on this action.

The librarian is verifying/following-up with the patron with questions re. whether the information provided is what the patron needs or not and what further information is needed.

I do this just with patrons I identify that the purpose of the need is in depth-research or any kind of project that requires follow up. For the rest of them I make "closure questions" with the intention that patrons let me know if they were satisfied.

In my personal experience the chat/e-mail communications are easier to give a reference service. E-mail are easier than chat because it is possible to take my time to reread and correct the answer that I am giving. For some patrons is better because they can print the instructions to follow them but some of them do not like to read a long answer no matter how useful it can be.

Using chat for users and librarians is excellent for quick reference because is the best way to enter, ask and leave.

In systems like the one I use, where you have to assist more than 3 or 4 people at the same time, in the same window, the reference can be complicated but patrons usually react well to this because all of them know they are several and just one person on the other side.

I am sure that in my experience everything is different because we don't have a physical collection and just assist patrons in person when teachers are working in the same building. This provokes that my services is always on distance and my work rhythm differs completely to the "in person" service.

Overview of the Reference Interview Process in the Contexts of Face-to-Face, Chat, and E-mail

Katz (2001) identified four phases of a successful reference interview:

1. Analyzing the Reference Question
2. Conducting a Good Reference Interview
3. Developing a Search Strategy
4. Delivering the Information

These are phases of a process and not steps in a procedure. A reference interview begins with analyzing the question, but analyzing the question requires the reference interview to begin. Westbrook (2006:254) identifies the "opening exchange" of the reference interview as the point at which the user locates the service on the library's Web site and decides to connect. This involves the user feeling welcome as well as recognizing that asking for reference assistance while working online is desirable.

Developing a search strategy requires the question analysis. Conducting a good reference interview, which involves the user by sharing search information and asking for the user's input, is essential for verifying the search strategy success, and for delivering the information.

Phase 1: Analyzing the Reference Question

Analyzing the reference question should always be done whether the librarian does a good reference interview or not. The reference interview enhances our success in analyzing the reference question correctly. We need to determine the subject, type, scope, depth, and context of the question in order to begin developing a search strategy:

- What was the actual question asked?
- What type of question was asked? For example, was it known item (holdings), directional/policies and procedures, ready-reference (short answer), specific-search, or research?
- Does the librarian know of an information source that will provide the information requested?
- What subject area, level, depth, or scope of information does the user seem to need? For example, elementary school earth sciences homework vs. postgraduate literature review of the latest liquid crystal technologies research.

- Given the nature of the question asked, what more do you need to know from the user?
- What questions will you need to ask the user in order to verify and clarify the reference question and the exact information needed?

In face-to-face reference interviewing, you can use nonverbal information to assess the user's age and therefore get a rough sense of the educational level of the materials required. Face-to-face nonverbal cues may indicate to the librarian the comfort level, time constraints, or urgency in asking the question, thereby giving a sense of how far to take additional questioning before the user will end the interaction from discomfort, lack of interest, or lack of time. You can also get a sense of the user's apparent satisfaction with the interview, search, and information sources as they are recommended. However, it is risky to make assumptions about subject, level, depth, and urgency of information needs based on a user's physical appearance alone. You may be working (as I have) with a 12-year-old postgraduate engineering student, a successful entrepreneur who buys her clothes from rummage sales and cuts her own hair, or a brand-new undergraduate who just finished 20 years in the army. It is always best to conduct a good reference interview to get needed information. Obviously, in order to analyze the question, you need to do a good reference interview, where you will also identify the information needs, seek additional information, clarify the question, and give feedback. Chapter 3 pursues this topic in virtual reference specific detail.

Interview Question 2

Face-to-face reference interview communications include eye contact, gestures, posture, facial expressions and tone of voice to convey information to the patron or for the librarian to gather information from the patron. I think that appropriate use of emoticons, grammar, and 'tone' of chat/email can emulate these non-verbal communications. Do you think these non-verbal communication modes can be emulated in chat or email reference? How? To what extent? What do you do personally? or What do you teach others to do?

KP: Some VR librarians are very good at "hearing" a patron's tone and using that to make the session more effective. I think this is easier when a librarian is completely comfortable with the technology of the VR software and confident in his or her reference skills. I also think it takes a positive attitude about VR and customer service in general. I've seen quite a few transcripts where I would say the librarian misinterpreted a patron's tone, and I think this is partly because some librarians just assume that online patrons are going to be rude. If they have that expectation, then the patron's tone may seem rude or uncooperative, even when that is not the patron's intention. I've also seen transcripts where the librarian has tried to use humor with a patron, and the patron has interpreted the message in a different way.

What I do, and what I teach my librarians to do is to be very polite, professional, and considerate with all patrons. It's fine, and often very effective, to let personality and informality show through by using emoticons, chat lingo, humor, etc., but I encourage librarians *never* to let their messages sound less formal than the patron's. For instance, if I have a student who is complaining about his or her assignment, I might write, "Yikes! That does sound hard. Let's see what we can find." If a patron writes a message that they clearly intend to be humorous, I'll send a :-) or write "lol!"

SM: In-person communication is obviously the preferred method for communication because of the nonverbal, audio, and other cues which accompany the words. Even on the phone you can use vocal tones and inflection to accompany the message. I don't think these can be emulated online so much as replaced by other types of communication which may fit better within the text chat environment. Online chat communication is very challenging for two reasons:

1. We only have the text message which can be read and interpreted in a variety of ways if not accompanied by the other cues.
2. Chat is a relatively new medium in which there are not clearly understood/ agreed-upon social norms about text language, spontaneous messages, and the variance in time frames between responses.

Some of our suggestions:

Use emoticons with discretion. Emoticons can be helpful with younger users who are used to using these for rapport building. Older users often find them annoying.

It helps to use more informal language than in person as well as to "think aloud" by typing things like "um . . . ," and "hmmm, let's think about this."

Take time to compliment the person, "That's an interesting question. Let's see what we can find on that." "Thank you for the clarification. That helps a lot."

User feedback indicates that when the librarian uses the customer's name and informal messages rather than scripted messages, the customer feels the librarian is more friendly. We suggest starting with an informal welcome which uses the person's screen name to establish a friendly rapport "Hi Diane. Welcome." This also helps with people who have not used the service to understand they are talking with a real person.

Inserting humor can be helpful to build rapport and help with the "friendly librarian" role we play. However, sarcasm often is read as a statement rather than an ironic remark. For this reason, sarcasm should be avoided.

We instruct staff to send frequent messages and not a lot of text per message. This helps to "continue" the conversation during gaps in time, update the person on the other end, and keep the conversation progressing with quick phrases back and forth. "Let me check on that." "Hang on . . ." We also instruct staff to send questions to elicit a response to keep the customer engaged in the conversation as well. "Let me know what you think." "Are you able to see. . . ."

PO: Of course, everything is typed in the chat sessions we do now, except pages we push. You do get a clue by how the question is phrased, or by the patience or impatience of the patron, and whether they share work that they may have already done on the question. Some people believe that it is good to use chat language and other mannerisms that may make us more approachable to youngsters. I have mixed feelings, as we emphasize that we are not just another chat room. We stick to library questions and homework questions, and we say that to kids who want to delve into the personal. Also, we have no time to digress when we are handling multiple patrons at one time.

Sometimes it is hard to convey to the patron that you are simply trying to home in on what he/she needs. Youngsters often think that the librarian who asks a lot of questions is just being difficult. I try to push pages to them and ask, "Is this what you need?" as a way of clarifying.

It is helpful to thank the patron for any clarifications they offer, to say things to encourage them in their explorations, to encourage them to come back again.

E-mail is more difficult than chat, because sometimes it takes a long time to exchange enough e-mails to settle on the question. To deal with this we just do a quick search, send, and ask the patron to get back to us with more clarification if needed.

JY: The Ask A Librarian service link takes the visitor to an e-mail form that asks whether the questioner is an adult or student and also asks for zip code. The form includes questions to help the patron think about what they are looking for. Examples include "Are you looking for a book, DVD, or magazine article? Do you know the time period, names of important people?"

KLR: Whether emoticons work depends on the software being used for chat reference and on the person on the other end of the chat (whether that person recognizes the emoticon is something the librarian can't control). AOL IM is much more flexible in allowing for emoticons; other chat software used in reference service isn't as flexible, and what is an attempt to be friendly and "approachable" ends up looking like mistyped characters, particularly if the patron isn't familiar with character-based emoticons.

Tone is another one that is extremely difficult to capture in a text-based medium—very often the patron is more interested in a quick response than in an indication of empathy or willingness to help.

Those seem to be assumed by the patron in chat reference—and that is a logical inference. We wouldn't be staffing the service if we weren't interested in helping. The biggest problem is when the help sought isn't appropriate to the service offered. It is exceedingly difficult to work through a complex topic and locate a wide variety of resources through chat. And that is an area of communication difficulty, what the librarian perceives as an attempt to help the student find a better method to get help is likely perceived by the student as not helping at all—especially if they have a very short deadline. A referral tends to go much more smoothly in person because they've seen you try to help them and understand the referral isn't an attempt to "shirk," but an honest attempt to make sure they do get what they need.

Grammar is another problem. When staffing a chat reference service you want to be able to "connect" with the patron, but also not be perceived as unqualified. Typically, I use plain English rather than try to use chat shorthand—in part because I never know who is on the other side of the chat. If it is someone who chats frequently, they still should be able to understand me, but if it is someone who isn't a big chat user, then using the shorthand adds an unnecessary level of complexity to the interaction. The major problem is to make sure that you don't use jargon, exactly the same problem librarians run into at the reference desk. Another issue is speed of response—using chat shorthand is faster, but it isn't as clear—especially for a librarian who may not use chat except when staffing the reference service.

LB: It is much faster to talk than to type. It is nice to have the transcript especially if you have to follow up with the patron. Having good scripts makes some of this easier.

JV: I guess I have to agree with most of this. The only thing I have a slightly different take on is that follow-up is harder for the librarian because the patron is looking at what's already been provided. I think this is true from the librarian's point of view. But I think most patrons (definitely *not* all patrons) don't need as much info as the librarian wants to give them. For example, a student may not have a clear idea in his or her mind what direction his/her paper is going to go in. Looking at what the librarian already provided can help with this, but it might need some time. So I think the most important thing for a librarian to do, even more important than, "Do you need more information?" is to issue an invitation to use the service again. If an hour goes by and the patron realizes they need something else, he/she can just hop back online. It isn't like having to schedule another trip to the library's reference desk, so it isn't as important to get *all* the information the first time around.

SH: I personally believe that it is possible to emulate the "tone" of the message that we send when using chat or e-mail in a reference interview. But not just how you might "sound" or how the user will be reading you is important; it is also necessary to consider the time between one message and its replay.

For example, if I received an e-mail and the "tone" of the user is urgent but I need to clarify the question, I add some information to let him know that my answer is not a wasting of time (for the user of course). Sometimes, if it is possible, I add a possible answer so the user can know that I might not have understand the question. This method has given me good responses, and they usually extend their explanation about their need.

In the other hand, the use of emoticons, at least here in my work, is not well seen by many people when responding to users, because it might be considered too familiar in the communication with the user. It is common to avoid "make bonding" to students in order to "sound" professional. However, personally I think there are some emoticons that can be appropriate to use—as I called them "the two basics," like :) : (.

The use of other expressions like ;) :P (and many others) tend to be more "familiar," and I actually try to not use them.

I don't think I can define an extension of the use on the emoticons because it will depend in the nature of the answer we choose, but mostly it is based on how the question was made, because we also are "readers" of our user's tone.

Phase 2: Conducting a Good Reference Interview

This is the phase of the reference interview where communication skills are most critical. ALA/RUSA "Guidelines for Behavioral Performance of Reference and Information Service Providers" advises reference librarians to:

- Be approachable or welcoming.
- Show appropriate interest in the user's question.
- Listen or otherwise pay attention.
- Clarify and verify by paraphrasing the user's question or ask open guiding questions if needed.
- Formulate a search strategy and share it with the user if appropriate.
- Instruct the user in the use of recommended reference sources, if needed.
- Follow-up. Check on the user's satisfaction with the interview process as well as with the recommended information sources.
- Conclude the interview. (Guidelines, 2004)

The 2004 edition recognizes that these guidelines apply equally to virtual reference. Ronan (2003a) also did an exemplary job of elucidating how these behavioral guidelines apply to virtual reference guidelines. The behavioral guidelines are keys to success for good reference interviews in virtual or face-to-face reference service:

1. Be approachable or welcoming.
2. Show appropriate interest in the user's question.
3. Listen or otherwise pay attention.
4. Clarify and verify by paraphrasing the user's question or ask open guiding questions if needed.
5. Formulate a search strategy and share it with the user if appropriate.
6. Follow up on the user's satisfaction.
7. Formally conclude the interview. (Ronan, 2003a)

Reference Interview Success Key 1: Be approachable or welcoming

Approachability in face-to-face reference service might be achieved by appropriate body language, location of service, eye contact, or appropriate tone of voice. It can be a challenge for some librarians to be approachable and welcoming enough without being too friendly. For others, behavior they feel is approachable may in fact not be comfortable for some users. One colleague of mine was famous for thinking she was smiling when in fact most people would look at her face and think she was merely serene, bored, or even dour. However, once students realized that she was an excellent reference librarian with very good source knowledge and was eager to work with them, they sought her out during her scheduled hours.

Face-to-face interactions may require some practice and self-monitoring to ensure that you are projecting the level of approachability and willingness to help that you mean to project during a reference interview. Practice and conscious use of appropriate body language, voice tones, etc., are essential. Face-to-face reference interview communications include eye contact, gestures, posture, facial expressions, tone of voice, and other nonverbal information that the librarian conveys to library users in order to seem approachable and welcoming, indicate willingness to help, and confirm listening and paying attention.

Virtual reference approachability begins with the usability and accessibility of the library's Web site and, specifically, the ease of navigation to, location of, and connection to the virtual reference service. Dee and Allen's research, reported in their article "A Survey of the Usability of Digital Reference Services on Academic Health Science Library Web Sites" (2006), clearly supports this concept. However, the usability and accessibility of the virtual reference service is not the only factor that affects whether users will make use of the service. This very important factor for virtual reference approachability is supported by other research and anecdotal accounts as well (e.g., Meola and Stormont, 2002; Ronan, 2003a; Ronan, 2003b; Lipow, 2003; Hirko and Ross, 2004; Guidelines, 2004)

For virtual reference librarians working in chat or e-mail, approachability and welcoming must be accomplished with words. Welcoming text can be as simple as, "Hello, I'm a librarian, how can I assist you?" or with added features such as inset photographs in chat sessions (depending on your software), or giving a name (depending on your policies). Some librarians will be comfortable using emoticons, such as :). Some will not. Appropriate use of emoticons, grammar, and "tone" of chat/e-mail can emulate face-to-face communications to a certain extent. However, the technology and consensus communications strategies used in providing virtual reference services require greater attention to textual cues and a greater requirement that the librarian deliberately communicate a welcoming persona—specifically, query to indicate listening and paying attention, confirm approachability, and otherwise converse. You cannot nod and smile; you must type "yes" and a smiley face or "yes" and some affirmative statement that welcomes queries, confirms, or otherwise converses. In chat reference, you must learn to type your responses in clear, thoughtful, but quickly typed text. You must learn to be self-reflective about what your typed words say about whether you are being approachable, interested, and attentive. You also must be aware of how approachable—usable and accessible—the virtual reference software seem to users.

Reference Interview Success Key 2: Show appropriate interest in the user's question

Face-to-face interest can be indicated by body language, such as nodding or moving to stand next to the user while using an information resource, as well as verbal responses indicating interest, such as "that is interesting . . . " as a prestatement before paraphrasing or asking open-ended questions to clarify and verify the question.

In chat or e-mail, interest must be indicated through words, whether typed individually or preset in the chat or e-mail software. Informal chatters use body language indicators such as "/me nods" or "*nods*." Paraphrasing or typing an open question that attempts to clarify and verify the user's question also shows appropriate interest. Remember, the virtual reference service user cannot see you nod or read your body language visually. In e-mail especially, slowness of response is almost always interpreted by the sender as lack of interest on the part of the receiver.

Reference Interview Success Key 3: Listen or otherwise pay attention

Listening and paying attention face-to-face is indicated primarily with body language—nodding—or making affirmative verbal responses.

In chat or e-mail, you will need to use text to show that you are continuing to monitor and read the user's typed questions. Typing a paraphrased question or typing appropriately gauged open-ended questions to clarify user questions may often be adequate. In the case of a long interaction, typing words that indicate that you understand what they are saying, or a body language indicator at the points in the interaction at which you would be nodding during a face-to-face interaction can be useful. Listening and remembering is potentially easier in chat and e-mail because the communication is in text on the screen and can be reread, copied, and pasted.

Reference Interview Success Key 4: Clarify and verify by paraphrasing the user's question or ask open guiding questions if needed

Neutral questioning (also called open-ended questioning), in which we try to elicit details about the respondent's information needs, and ethnographic interviewing, in which we try to elicit details about the respondent's experiences, are good models for the interviews we need to conduct to provide successful reference services. (Crichton and Kinash, 2003; Ronan, 2003a; Ronan, 2003b; Lipow, 2003; Hirko and Ross, 2004; Meola and Stormont, 2002; Ross, Nilsen, and Dewdney, 2002; Rollman and Parente, 2001; Nofsinger, 1999; Dewdney, 1986)

In order to analyze the reference question—whether face-to-face, in chat, or e-mail—the librarian must query specifically by asking open-ended questions regarding the educational level of materials required; determine the user's comfort level, time limits, urgency, and satisfaction with the process at any given point; and paraphrase the user response as a check to understanding. For example, the librarian might ask:

- What kind of information do you want to find? Do you need in-depth, technical, specific information, or would you prefer a general source on that topic?
- Is this for a homework assignment? For what class? Can you describe the assignment?
- Does this seem like what you need?

Face-to-face, you'll ask the question. You'll need to have good short-term memory and keep track of the user's answers during the interaction.

In chat and e-mail, you'll have the advantage of being able to cut and paste the user's questions and make adjustments to the wording. You can also refer back to the text of the interaction to make sure you understood what was typed or to refresh your memory during a long interaction.

E-mail reference interviews are often minimal, probably because of the lack of speed of turn-taking in the interaction. Many libraries use a form that encourages at least a cursory reference interview for e-mail reference questions. Users complete a short survey that places their question in subject and scope context.

Reference Interview Success Key 5: Formulate a search strategy and share it with the user, if appropriate

Not everyone thinks it is necessary to share the search strategy with the user. However, if you are assisting the user in doing research, the user will need to know what you recommend and how to begin their research. Even when answering an apparently simple question, librarians should cite the sources of the information they give to a user, e.g., you might say or type, "According to http://www.senate.gov, your State Senator is X and she is up for election in X," or "I'm looking at the Million Dollar Directory volume X and it says that X company is located in X." Face-to-face, it is appropriate to explain and show users what you are doing to assist them or get them started. Instruct users in the use of recommended information resources and search tools if that is your library's policy (as it is in many academic libraries), or ask users if they would like you to teach them how to search the resource or use a search tool.

It is always acceptable during a virtual reference interview to invite the user to come into the library for additional instruction, or to access sources that are building-use only, or to go to tutorials online for instruction (on Web-based sources, for example). However, keep in mind this thought from Buckley's article "Golden Rule Reference: Face-to-Face and Virtual" (2006). Most people using virtual reference are doing so because they do not want to have to physically get up and go to the library, and they would prefer that the information be received online as well. In chat or e-mail, instruction requires you to be very detailed and give step-by-step explanations on how to search a given resource. Face-to-face, you may be able to demonstrate or "show" the user what to do rather than using verbal instructions.

Reference Interview Success Key 6: Follow-up on the user's satisfaction

Verify the user's satisfaction with the interview process as well as with the recommended information resources.

Face-to-face, you may simply observe that the user is actively using an information resource, or you may ask, "How is that working for you?"

In chat and e-mail, you must ask or otherwise solicit affirmation from the user. E-mail is often used as a follow-up for chat reference service. Follow-up within chat reference is harder for the librarian because the user may not be paying attention to the chat if they have gone off to look at the information already provided, and the librarian may not know how to contact the user without additional personal information having been provided. Follow-up can be easier for the virtual reference user because they initiated the reference process and can return to it easily. Also, the answer is recorded with text instructions and directions that they may print, rather than oral instructions that they must remember after leaving the librarian.

Reference Interview Success Key 7: Formally conclude the interview

Especially in chat, it can be difficult to decide when the reference interview is over. How is the reference interview concluded? Does the user seem satisfied with the response to his/her question? How do you know? What do users do or say face-to-face? What do they say in chat? In chat or e-mail reference, it is important to conclude the interview formally. Type a query, such as "Is that what you needed to know?" or "Do you have enough to get started?" It is always important to end a reference interview by offering additional assistance if the user might need it, regardless of whether you are interviewing face-to-face or virtually.

Chapter 3 continues this discussion with more detail on specific communications skills and knowledge needed for good virtual reference interviewing.

Phase 3: Developing a Search Strategy

Developing a search strategy means applying source knowledge, modifying the search based on the interview responses, and formulating search or source alternatives. Essentially, you need to decide, consider, or discover:

1. Into which subject area(s) does the question generally fall?
2. Do you need to provide a single fact answer, or assist the user in in-depth research? For example, is this a known item (holdings), directional/policies and procedures, ready-reference (short answer), specific-search, or research question?
3. Do you know of a reference book or database that will answer the question? Will that book or database be a good place for the user to begin or continue their research?
4. Which information source(s) will you use first? Why?
5. Type or write down the keywords and Boolean operators you would use if searching a database (fee, free, Web-accessible, or library use only), Web search engine, or library catalog.
6. How do you plan to deliver the information to the user?

Search Strategy Question 1: Into which subject area(s) does the question generally fall?

Regardless of the reference mode, you will need to have solid reference and some core subject source knowledge. At this stage, you may conclude that you don't know enough to continue and refer the user to another librarian subject-specialist or to external resources, then monitor that the user was able to make use of the referrals. The subject area will guide you to the information sources you will recommend or use in answering the question. Choosing the best source that you know of for a particular subject area is ideal. For example, in a chat reference session I did with KnowItNow24/7 (http://knowitnow.org/), a user asked, "My fingernails are falling out, why would they do that?" I was able to refer the user directly from the chat session to the MetroHealthLine nurse service, a medical information service through a local hospital system. If that had not been available, the best I could have done in that situation would have been to send her to the

Medlineplus.gov site with basic keyword search instructions for the encyclopedia and topics areas, and a firm recommendation that she consult a medical professional. The latter strategy would work face-to-face as well. If the professional medical referral had not been available, we could have remained in chat while exploring the information available from Medlineplus.gov to see if it is what she needed, and if not to consider alternative sources. Medical questions almost always require tactful recommendations that the user also consult a medical professional.

Search Strategy Question 2: Do you need to provide a single fact answer or assist the user in in-depth research?

In the former case, you will need to know the best source to answer the question and be able to report the source of the answer to the user. In the latter case, you may need to recommend multiple sources or plan for long-term interaction with the user as they progress through the project.

Search Strategy Question 3: Do you know of a reference book or database that will answer the question? Will that book or database be a good place for users to begin or continue their research?

During face-to-face reference service, you can accompany users to a source, determine together whether it is going to answer their question, teach them how to search for more information, and follow up with other sources or information needs that emerge during the original interview and search process. During virtual reference service, you must be explicit and perhaps more comprehensive in search strategies and making a first choice of sources, as there are fewer opportunities for follow-up or co-browsing sources. Most important, you must explain to the user, by typing in text, what search strategies you will employ and how the user can proceed from those strategies. Ideally, share the search strategy with the user, then attempt the search for them or teach them how to do the search or, better yet, work on the search collaboratively. Reassure the user that he/she can return for additional assistance as it becomes necessary. Repeat as needed.

Search Strategy Question 4: Which information source(s) will you use first? Why?

Virtual reference service requires broad awareness of available sources of information, as well as strong functional knowledge of available information-finding tools. Some librarians are most comfortable with print resources for most questions; some are comfortable referring to electronic resources immediately. What is most important is that you choose the source that is going to be best for the user. Some may prefer to use a print telephone book or dictionary rather than <u>Anywho.com</u> or <u>Dictionary.com</u>. Virtual reference users tend to want electronic resources—especially those that they can connect to directly and get full-text information. However, that is not always the best tool for them. Some information is not available freely on the Web, may not be accessible through the library, or may not even be available in electronic format. This is especially an issue when we are looking at any kind of historical or genealogical research that requires access to archival records or back issues of journals.

If you do not know a specific source where the information might be obtained, you may then want to search the library catalog or possibly a Web search engine or other finding tool to locate an appropriate information source.

Search Strategy Question 5: Type or write down the keywords and Boolean operators you would use if searching a database (fee, free, Web-accessible, or library-use-only), Web search engine, or library catalog.

Face-to-face, you may skip this step if the user can see you type in the search or if you are verbally instructing the user to type the search. But it can be very useful for the user if you can hand them a piece of paper with a good solid search statement to use in their searching.

In virtual reference, typing the search that you will use for them, or that you recommend they use in a database they have access to, is essential to ensure that users knows that you are working on their question and so there is a record of what you already did that they can refer to if they are going to need additional assistance. Explaining how and what you are searching on as you work with users indicates that you are working on their question and are interested and attentive. It will also make it more likely that they will be able to explain what was already done in their search if they return for additional assistance.

Search Strategy Question 6: How do you plan to deliver the information to the user?

It takes practice and experience, but most good reference librarians command knowledge of the most useful and accessible resources available to their users. Most of us learn our own libraries very thoroughly. In virtual reference you'll need to choose sources that are not only accessible to you where you are physically or virtually located but that are also accessible to the user.

Phase 4: Delivering the Information

Chapter 4 explores the reference skills and knowledge required for good reference interviewing, with specifics for virtual reference as well as policies, procedures, copyright, and licensing issues affecting information delivery options in virtual reference. The technical competencies discussed in Chapter 2 are also essential for information delivery.

Information delivery ultimately involves:

- selecting information sources,
- choosing formats,
- sending or otherwise giving the information to the user, and
- following up and verifying the success of the whole process.

This is the stage at which source knowledge becomes essential. It is important to be aware of the kinds and sources of information in general. But more important is to be aware of what kinds and sources of information are accessible to your library users both face-to-face and virtually.

During face-to-face reference interviewing, you can interact physically with information sources in cooperation with the library user. Virtual reference service information delivery must take into account the sources users have access to from their current location. Specific questions need to be asked:

- Can you come in to the library to view books or articles that are not available through the Web?
- Can you receive faxes?
- Can you receive e-mailed attachments? Are there any restrictions on which file formats (e. g., some e-mail systems will not allow .html or .doc), size limits, etc.?
- Can you make use of file-sharing?
- Can you download from Web or ftp?

Competencies for Virtual Reference Librarians

Reference librarian competencies, and specifically those competencies required to excel at offering virtual reference services, are frequent topics for research and practical articles in the library and information sciences literature. The competencies identified for this handbook are synthesized from a review of the library literature (Nofsinger, 1999; Meola and Stormont, 2002; Smith, 2002; Ronan, 2003a; Ronan, 2003b; Lipow, 2003; Hirko and Ross, 2004; Guidelines, 2004; DREI, 2004; Salem, Balraj and Lilly, 2004; Lindbloom, Yackle, Burhans, Peters, and Bell, 2006; Westbrook, 2006) and e-mail conversations with virtual reference librarians. The competencies are organized according to technical, communications, and reference skills and knowledge, and whether they are basic or advanced.

The balance of this handbook focuses on achieving these competencies. Chapter 2 details technical competencies, Chapter 3 discusses communications competencies, and Chapter 4 addresses reference competencies. Each competency is described in terms of learning goals—what the learner needs to be able to know or do—and performance objectives—what the learner needs to be able to do with what is learned.

Simply stated, the virtual reference librarian needs comfort (with the technology), confidence (with the communications), and competence (in reference skills and knowledge).

Self-Assessment Activities

The self-assessment activities are also available at http://www.kovacs.com/ns/ chatrefbook/chatrefbook.html. These are simple statements of the competencies—skills and knowledge for virtual reference librarians—discussed in Chapters 2–4. How would you rate your own current competencies with regard to these skills and knowledge? Try this again after you read Chapters 2–4 and have completed the Learning Activities in those chapters. Consider how your skills and knowledge have grown or changed. Interactive versions of the self-assessment activities are available on the companion Web site.

Definition of terms used in describing learning goals and performance objectives:

- "Demonstrate awareness of" means the learner knows and can explain to others that a given concept, skill, or activity exists and that the learner can find out more about it.
- "Understanding of" means the learner can write or talk effectively about a given concept, skill, or activity and apply it to appropriate situations. Understanding exceeds mere awareness in that it "is a psychological process related to an abstract or physical object, such as, person, situation and message whereby one is able to think about it and use concepts to deal adequately with that object"—http://en.wikipedia.org/wiki/Understanding—as opposed to just knowing that the concept, skill, or activity exists.
- "Ability to" means that the learner is able to actually perform an activity or identified skill.

- "Detailed functional knowledge" means that the learner is able to actually perform an activity or identified skill, and to teach others; the learner can write or talk in detail about the underlying concept of an identified skill or activity and apply it to appropriate situations

Technical Competencies (T)	Demonstrate awareness of	Understanding of	Ability to	Detailed functional knowledge of
T1.1 how to type on a computer keyboard and make use of other related input devices (e.g., mouse, trackball, touchpad, etc.)				
T1.2 how to work with multiple software applications on a computer with multiple windows, to move appropriately between windows/applications, and to move quickly and mindfully between multiple activities—chatting, searching print or electronic sources, etc. (minimal multi-tasking)				
T1.3 how to access the Internet, use Internet e-mail, connect to Web sites (e.g., using URLs, etc.)				
T1.4 how to use at least one Web browser				
T1.5 basic technologies that any given virtual reference service user may or may not be using, have access to, or be limited by				
T1.6 chat software specifics for a given system you are going to be using.				
T1.7 how to connect to and chat through a Web-based chat software, Instant Messaging tool, etc.				
T1.8 the options for document or information delivery				
T1.9 sending files as attachments in e-mail				
T1.10 file transfer options (e.g., Instant Messaging, ftp, Web posting)				
T1.11 common computer file formats e.g., .txt, .doc .html .gif .jpg .mpg, .pdf, etc.				
T1.12 local e-mail system and limitations				
T1.13 other e-mail systems and limitations				
T1.14 how and where to download, install, and use toolbars, search engines, plug-ins, and other helpful browser extensions				
T1.15 Ability to use a document scanner to scan print materials to be faxed and/or saved for transfer to the user (e.g., send as attachments by e-mail, file transfer options)				

Communications Competencies (C)	Demonstrate awareness of	Understand-ing of	Ability to	Detailed functional knowledge of
C1.1 how to learn and continue learning technical, communications, and reference skill and knowledge				
C1.2 how, why, and when to use good reference interviewing skills and techniques				
C1.3 Ability to empathize with virtual reference users during a virtual reference interview, and to understand something of the culture and social environment of the Internet				
C1.4 how to explain library and research processes without using library jargon				
C1.5 how to imagine and project a professional persona as part of library participation in the Internet Community—"library space" on the Web				
C1.6 how to provide information without making value judgments, to maintain and project professional objectivity				
C1.7 how to read carefully and quickly, the text typed by a library user and displayed on a computer monitor—communicating to the user that you are "listening"				
C1.8 how and why to "be there" for the user—avoid "silence"				
C1.9 how and when to teach or instruct during a virtual reference transaction				
C1.10 how and when to provide follow-up, referrals, or to request consultations with other professionals				
C1.11 how to work with multiple users in a virtual reference only environment				

Reference Competencies (R)	Demonstrate awareness of	Understand-ing of	Ability to	Detailed functional knowledge of
R1.1 how to be approachable, to maintain and project a welcoming and enthusiastic reference service attitude through text-based communications				
R1.2 how, when, and why to apply organizational policies relevant to any given user of a specific virtual reference service				
R1.3 ready-reference sources of information, such as encyclopedias, almanacs, indices, bibliographies and standard reference works in print and electronic formats				
R1.4 the best or core reference sources available in print and electronic formats, and of the range of information resources that may be used in the delivery of reference services for selected subjects and general reference				
R1.5 how to conduct good reference interviews, to analyze reference questions using knowledge of the structures, organization, and accessibility of information in print and electronic formats				
R1.6 how, when, and why to evaluate information resources for their appropriateness in level, scope, and format for a given user				
R1.7 how to develop effective and flexible search strategies including keyword and Boolean searching in library catalogs, licensed databases, and Web search engines (and know when to use advanced search options)				
R1.8 the scope and limitations of Web search engines				
R1.9 how to perform advanced searches in at least one major Web search engine				
R1.10 the scope and limitations of and the ability to use freely accessible Web Reference Tools				

(continued)

Reference Competencies (R) (Continued)	Demonstrate awareness of	Understand-ing of	Ability to	Detailed functional knowledge of
R1.11 how and why to evaluate information quality of Web published information, but also to think critically about all sources of information				
R1.12 the fee-based or licensed databases accessible to both the virtual reference librarian and any given user of virtual reference services				
R1.13 how and where to search local holdings information for print and electronic resources				
R1.14 how and where to search the catalogs of other libraries and library organizations				
R1.15 how and when to apply the available options for appropriate information referrals				

References and Recommended Readings

Buckley, Chad E. 2006. "Golden Rule Reference: Face-to-Face and Virtual." *The Reference Librarian* 93:129–136.

Crichton, Susan, and Shelley Kinash. 2003. "Virtual Ethnography: Interactive Interviewing Online as Method." *Canadian Journal of Learning and Technology* 29 no. 2(Spring) http://www.cjlt.c/Acontent/vol29.2/cjlt29–2 art–5.html

Dee, Cheryl, and Maryellen Allen. 2006. "A Survey of the Usability of Digital Reference Services on Academic Health Science Library Web Sites." *The Journal of Academic Librarianship* 32 no. 1:69–78.

Dewdney, P. 1986. *The Effects of Training Reference Librarians in Interview Skills: A Field Experiment.* Doctoral Dissertation, University of Toronto. Advisor: Catherine Ross.

Digital Reference Education Inititiative (DREI) Draft Competencies for Digital Reference. 2004. http://drei.syr.edu/item_list.cfm?NavID=9

Ford, Charlotte. 2003. "An Exploration of the Differences between Face-to-Face and Computer-Mediated Reference Interactions." Ph.D. Dissertation, Indiana University, School of Library and Information Science. Advisor: Stephen Harter.

Guidelines for Behavioral Performance of Reference and Information Service Providers. 2004. Reference and User Services Association, American Library Association. http://www.ala.org/al/Arus/Arusaprotools/referenceguide/guidelinesbehavioral.htm

Hirko, Buff, and Mary B. Ross. 2004. *Virtual Reference Training: The Complete Guide to Providing Anytime Anywhere Answers.* Chicago: ALA Editions.

Katz, William A. 2002. *Introduction to Reference Work, Volume I.* 8th ed. Columbus, Ohio: McGraw-Hill.

Lankes, R. David; Joseph Janes; Linda C. Smith; and Christina M. Finneran (eds). 2004. *Virtual Reference Experience: Integrating Theory Into Practice.* New York: Neal-Schuman.

Lindbloom, Mary-Carol; Anna Yackle; Skip Burhans; Tom Peters; and Lori Bell. 2006. "Virtual Reference: A Reference Question is a Reference Question . . . Or is Virtual Reference a New Reality? New Career Opportunities for Librarians." *The Reference Librarian* 93:3–22.

Lipow, Anne G. 2003. *The Virtual Reference Librarian's Handbook.* New York: Neal-Schuman.

Luo, Lili (<pkulili@yahoo.com>. research in progress), a Ph.D student at UNC-Chapel Hill, is running a survey of virtual reference librarians asking them to prioritize the competencies required for chat reference librarians.

Meola, Marc, and Sam Stormont. 2002. *Starting and Operating Live Virtual Reference Services.* New York: Neal-Schuman.

Nilsen, Kirsti. 2005. "Virtual versus Face-to-Face Reference: Comparing Users' Perspectives on Visits to Physical and Virtual Reference Desks in Public and Academic Libraries." World Library and Information Congress, 71st IFLA General Conference and Council, August 14-18, 2005, Oslo Norway. www.ifla.org/IV/ifla71/papers/027e-Nilsen.pdf.

Nofsinger, Mary M. 1999. "Training and Retraining Reference Professionals: Core Competencies for the 21st Century." *The Reference Librarian* 64:9–19.

Parkhurst, C. A. 2002. "Supporting the Remote User of Licensed Resources." In Curtis, D., ed. *Attracting, Educating and Serving Remote Users Through the Web*. New York: Neal-Schuman: 197–226.

Parus, D. J. 1996. "The Reference Interview: Communication and the Patron." *The Katherine Sharp Review* no. 2(Winter) http://alexia.lis.uiuc.edu/review.old/winter1996/

Pomerantz, J.; L. Luo; and C. R. McClure. 2006. "Peer Review of Chat Reference Transcripts: Approaches and Strategies." *Library and Information Science Research* 28 no. 1 (Spring):24–48.

Pomerantz, J.; S. Nicolson; Y. Belanger; and R. D. Lankes. In press. "The Current State of Digital Reference: Validation of a General Reference Model through a Survey of Digital Reference Services." *Information Processing and Management.*

Pomerantz, J. 2005. "A Conceptual Framework and Open Research Questions for Chat-Based Reference Service." *Journal of the American Society for Information Science and Technology* 56 no. 12 (October):1288–1302

Rollman, J. Brian, and Fredrick Parente. 2001. "Relation of Statement Length and Type and Type of Chat Room to Reciprocal Communication on the Internet." *CyberPsychology and Behavior* 4 no. 5:617–622.

Ronan, Jana S. 2003a. "The Reference Interview Online." *Reference & User Services Quarterly* 43 no. 1 (Fall):43–47.

Ronan, Jana S. 2003b. *Chat Reference: A Guide to Live Virtual Reference Services*. Westport, Conn.: Libraries Unlimited.

Ross, Catherine Sheldrick; Kirsti Nilsen; and Patricia Dewdney. 2002. *Conducting the Reference Interview: A How-To-Do-It Manual for Librarians*. New York: Neal-Schuman.

Ross, Catherine Sheldrick. 2003. "The Reference Interview: Why It Needs to be Used in Every (Well Almost Every) Reference Transaction." *Reference & User Services Quarterly* 43 no. 1 (Fall):37–43.

Salem, Joseph A. Jr.; Leela Balraj; and Erica B. Lilly. 2004. "Real-Time Training for Virtual Reference." In Lankes, R. David; Joseph Janes; Linda C. Smith; and Christina M. Finneran (eds). *The Virtual Reference Experience: Integrating Theory into Practice*. New York: Neal-Schuman:121–138.

Smith, Linda C. 2002. "Education for Digital Reference Services." Digital Reference Research Symposium, August 2–3, 2002, Harvard University, Cambridge, Mass. http://leep.lis.uiuc.edu/fall02/lis404lea/drseducation.html

Squire, Kurt, and Constance Steinkuehler. 2005. "Meet the Gamers." *Library Journal* 130 no. 7:38.

Virtual Reference Desk Conference. 2003. Part 4: Staffing & Training. Online Proceedings http://www.vrd.org/conferences/VRD2003/proceedings/#Staffing%20&%20Training

Ward, David. 2003. "Measuring the Completeness of Reference Transactions in Online Chats." *Reference & User Services Quarterly* 44 no. 1:46–58.

Westbrook, Lynn. 2006. "Virtual Reference Training: The Second Generation." *College & Research Libraries* 67 no. 3 (May):249–59.

Chapter 2

Acquire and Improve Technical Skills and Knowledge for Virtual Reference

> *Text-based chat requires ease with QWERTY keyboards. If a potential virtual reference service provider lacks typing skills, he or she must acquire them prior to beginning either training or delivery of service. . . . multitasking and online chat skills, require practice in order to achieve expertise . . . Knowledge of technical troubleshooting and software features . . . the training raised the awareness of the need for competency in these areas . . .*
>
> (Hirko and Ross, 2004:11)

The technical competencies essential or desirable for virtual reference librarians to acquire or to improve on are the foundation of virtual reference service provision. Virtual reference service is built on a technical infrastructure. The Internet, the World Wide Web, e-mail, Web chat, Instant Messaging, and all the associated supportive technology and software are the environment in which virtual reference librarians work.

Face-to-face reference service is built on a foundation of a physical building, and a meeting within that physical building. The physical building contains the library's print collection (and access to electronic information resources). Within that physical building, the reference librarian and the library user interact physically with these resources. The reference librarian and the library user must know how to locate and travel to the library building. The reference librarian must be aware of how the information resources are organized, where they are stored, how they are retrieved (e.g., pages, open circulation, closed stacks, rental, library cards, etc.) and how to search or otherwise make use of them. The reference librarian must also interact with the library user to offer reference service, encourage the library user to use the reference service, and then to identify, search for, and otherwise match the library user's information need with available information sources.

Virtual reference librarians must be able to do all of the above and more within a virtual environment that is defined by the technology. Virtual reference librarians and virtual reference service users must know how to locate and navigate to the virtual space where they can meet, identify, search, and match both print and electronic information sources to the information needs of the user, within the context of that virtual space. Technical competencies are the skills and knowledge virtual reference librarians must acquire in order to do this.

The technical competencies for virtual librarians discussed in the following are not intended to be a comprehensive list, but rather are a consensus of those deemed essential and desirable by experienced virtual reference librarians and researchers. Each competency is described in terms of learning goals—the skills and knowledge to be learned—and performance objectives—what the learner needs to be able to do with what is learned. Some of the basic skills and knowledge have a recommended advanced level. These are discussed within the general competency description. Each competency in turn is more fully described, with tips, advice, and ideas for learning, along with learning activities that might be used to test and build each competency. The learning activities are also available on the handbook's companion Web site.

Acquiring and improving technical competencies is an ongoing process. In "Training and Retraining Reference Professionals: Core Competencies for the 21st Century," Nofsinger (1999:13–14) reinforces the idea that we must make time to acquire and improve our technical skills:

> In regard to reference training, it is no longer possible to train librarians once and then expect them to provide ongoing satisfactory service to users. Instead, librarians must be trained and re-trained, again and again, as technologies change and new electronic resources become available. . . . Reference training must also ensure that librarians assume the role of consultant and teacher. . . . In order to develop this level of expertise, librarians must allocate adequate time to study, explore, and maintain their electronic skills—despite other responsibilities.

Interview Question 3

I think that chat reference librarians need to be able to:

- type accurately and quickly
- read fluently in English including local or regional dialects (and other languages if that service is provided)
  be articulate and detailed in writing details of information location and retrieval.

To practice these skills the best thing that librarians can do is to get online and begin chatting and practicing. I recommend simple Internet messaging and role-playing with colleagues and friends to practice. Use of the specific chat software being used by the organization they are working for is also important but the core skills are facility with typing/written/synchronous communication as opposed to face-to-face core skills of being verbally articulate and verbal listeners (rather than readers). Do you agree? How would you encourage new librarians or librarians just beginning to offer chat reference to become facile with the communication mode? Do you have any role-play exercises that you'd be willing to share? (I will cite you if I use these).

KP: I agree with your qualifications. I think one of the misunderstandings about chat is that it is difficult to communicate using it. One only needs to see people not just chatting—but using the even more stripped-down communication form of text-messaging—to realize how effective it can be. Many librarians I talk to—even those who are currently doing VR—talk about "chat lingo" and how all the kids use it and it is impossible to know what they're talking about. In my experience, patrons use very few abbreviations that someone with just a rough idea about chat lingo cannot understand.

I do encourage librarians to "practice" chatting. In our training sessions, when we do the hands-on part, we forbid them to try to stump each other with impossible reference questions, but encourage them just to have a conversation back and forth about what they had for lunch, how many pets they have, or what they'll be doing when they get home. We encourage them to just send each other Web sites they like, rather than trying to find the exact resource to answer to a question. We've found that starting by stressing chat skills rather than librarian skills keeps librarians more comfortable, and keeps the focus on the method of VR.

My librarians also chat with each other during shifts, and I think this "practice" helps them with patrons too. Often, our chats are about the questions we're getting and the resources we're using—but when things get a little slow, conversation turns to movies, food, pets, you name it (my librarians work from home, so e-mail and chat is their only form of communication with each other). I love to see the quick messages running up the chat screen, and I think it really helps make them more comfortable chatting in sessions as well.

SM: I also think that online reference requires that the librarian be interested in working on written and online communication. Some librarians do not like the format and will develop morale problems when working in this environment.

We find training works well when you have a veteran librarian working with a beginner. We also find that providing samples of transcripts for librarians to read helps them to get ideas for improving their online communication. Having staff come together and talk about their online experiences and what they have learned also improves their performance.

PO: I think the above (typing, etc.) is true to an extent, but the old reference skills are most critical, that is, locating information quickly and accurately, of heading in the right direction to get the answer (this is the well-aimed-dart approach), rather than floundering through all possible Google hits. It is important to be at ease with many databases, so you can find information, and also communicate to the patron how to find it and how to handle the source you send. It is important to be tactful. Also, it is important to generally have good computer skills and Windows skills. The librarian should be comfortable multitasking. Some staff are not comfortable opening more than one session at a time.

JY: Typing quickly is not as important as typing accurately.

KLR: Since I've been chat coordinator at Kent State, we haven't really done any of this. Generally I meet with folks new to our chat service to get them started and try to get them comfortable with the software. Beyond that, I tend to throw them to the wolves. There really isn't a lot I can think of that will adequately prepare them for the variety of chat transactions they will experience other than actually going on and giving it a shot. You also have to take into account that different individuals have different comfort levels—some of us type much faster and can handle answering two or three questions simultaneously, some of us cannot. In a service like OhioLINK's, there is sufficient staffing that those skill differences can be accommodated—in a single provider service, things might not be as flexible. I also think students, though they tend to get impatient sometimes, are actually multitasking too, so speed of response may not always be the first thing they care about (though sometimes it is very clear that it is).

LB: The software is changing so often and as more and more libraries move from VR to instant messaging or offering both, the skills transfer fairly well. I encourage new librarians or those unfamiliar with chat to get an instant messaging account and IM with their friends or even their teen kids. Role-playing and practice with other librarians is very important too and builds confidence. In the InfoEyes project, we set every librarian up with a mentor who would practice with them until they felt comfortable. Even after the practice, the librarian could contact the mentor with questions.

JV: I definitely agree that core skills are more important than knowledge of the software. That can be learned quickly. The core skills are harder to develop. I think doing chat reference is the best way to develop them, but spending time online and chatting in other situations is a good way to get used to the communication medium as well. The only caveat I would offer is that "type accurately" stresses people out. They want to correct all their mistakes. Most chat users know that occasional typos happen and they don't worry about them at all. It's hard for librarians to not type with perfect grammar and spelling and punctuation but I think most users, especially younger users, don't expect this.

SH: I agree with all of them. I can't imagine a reference service provider (even nonvirtual) not having this skills.

I just like to point out that being "quick" is not necessarily a good thing when using chat, because our patrons don't always read quickly. It is important to type quickly when writing an e-mail because it will take less time to answer something.

I don't necessarily agree with the role-play. First, because it is not a common practice in our country to do this. The common practice is just doing it for real. But, yes, practice with the software you have to use, it is much better in order to get those skills and be fluent in its manageability. However, just chatting with friends or family using the common products of messenger can be helpful to improve them.

I would strongly recommend to read a lot. It is more important to know how to structure a sentence, several ideas, and lots of paragraphs when we are giving this service than the physical communication skills per se.

Technical Competencies for Virtual Reference Librarians

- T1.1 Ability to type on a computer keyboard and make use of other related input devices (mouse, trackball, touchpad, etc.)
- T1.2 Ability to work with multiple software applications on a computer with multiple windows, to move appropriately between windows/applications, and to move quickly and mindfully between multiple activities—chatting, searching print or electronic sources, etc. (minimal multitasking)

- T1.3 Detailed functional knowledge of how to access the Internet, use Internet e-mail, and connect to Web sites
- T1.4 Detailed functional knowledge of at least one Web browser
- T1.5 Demonstrate awareness of the basic technologies that any given virtual reference service user may or may not be using, have access to, or be limited by
- T1.6 Demonstrate awareness of the chat software specifics for a given system you are going to be using then develop
  - o T1.6.a Detailed functional knowledge of the specific chat software used by your library or other organization for chat reference
- T1.7 Demonstrate awareness of how to connect to and chat through Web-based chat software, Instant Messaging, etc.
- T1.8 Demonstrate awareness of the options for document or information delivery
- T1.9 Demonstrate awareness of sending files as attachments in e-mail
  - o T1.9.a Detailed functional knowledge of sending files as attachments in e-mail
- T1.10 Demonstrate awareness of and the ability to make use of file transfer options (e.g., Instant Messaging, ftp, Web posting)
- T1.11 Demonstrate awareness of common computer file formats (e.g., .txt, .doc .html .gif .jpg .mpg, .pdf)
  - o T1.11.a Detailed functional knowledge of common computer file formats
- T1.12 Demonstrate awareness of the local e-mail system and limitations
  - o T1.12.a Detailed functional knowledge of the specific e-mail software used by your library or library organization
- T1.13 Demonstrate awareness of other e-mail systems and limitations
- T1.14 Demonstrate awareness of options to download, install, and use toolbars, search engines, plug-ins, and other helpful browser extensions.
  - o T1.14.a Ability to download, install, and use browser extensions, and similar helper programs
- T1.15 Ability to use a document scanner to scan print materials to be faxed and/or saved for transfer to the user (e.g., send as attachments by e-mail, file transfer options)

T1.1 Ability to type on a computer keyboard and make use of other related input devices (e.g., mouse, trackball, touchpad)

For conducting virtual reference interviews, you will need to be very comfortable typing and reading on the computer screen. This requires good typing skills and comfort in communicating in text and reading online.

Because the technology allows for a reference interview to occur in chat transactions, there is no excuse for overlooking the reference interview, yet in the Library Visit Study, 56% of these transactions made no attempt to interview the patrons, even worse than the 49% avoidance of interviews in face-to-face transactions. Why do librarians conducting chat transaction overlook the interview in chat?"

(Nilsen, 2005: 7)

The answer to this question may very well be that virtual reference librarians are not yet entirely comfortable typing and communicating with their fingers. Typing—communicating with your fingers—is how you communicate in performing virtual reference service. Whether chatting or using e-mail to answer reference questions, typing—sometimes called "keyboarding"—is the underlying action. In order to be able to communicate with virtual reference service users, you must be able to type quickly and accurately using a computer keyboard. An old-fashioned, but sensible, term for this is "touch-typing." The standard "qwerty" keyboard has a "home row" and you learn to type by memorizing and practicing which fingers go on which keys of the "home row" (The "asdf" keys are covered by the left hand from pinky to index finger and "jkl" keys are covered by the right hand from index finger to pinky) and which additional keys each finger is responsible for. If you can hunt and peck quickly and accurately that is fine, but touch-typing is preferable (and faster).

Learning Activity 2–1 links to some very good Web-based typing practice tools that are free to use, but some people may prefer to take formal typing lessons or use commercial typing tutorial software. I will always thank Miss Harper, my typing teacher at Franklin Center High School, Franklin Grove, Illinois (http://www.franklingroveil.org/), who taught me well and motivated me to communicate with my fingers. Being able to type almost as fast as I can talk has been a benefit not only while working my way through college, but is now even more useful when I teach online or do chat or e-mail reference. Ultimately, practice is the best way to learn and improve typing skills. I recommend that anyone who is going to do chat reference professionally also spend time chatting informally. Informal chatting is good practice for typing as well as for becoming comfortable and articulate with this mode of communication. Instant Messaging (IM) is the easiest way to practice, and some people find that it becomes a significant part of their social lives. Learning Activity 2–2 introduces some options for chat typing practice using Instant Messaging software. You may also IM me at diane.kovacs@gmail.com (Gtalk), SaintsMrsDi (AOL), or diane@kovacs.com (MSN or Yahoo chat) if you would like to say hello and practice communicating with your fingers.

The Learning Activities are also available at http://www.kovacs.com/ns/chatrefbook/chatrefbook.html

Learning Activity 2–1: Typing Practice Sites on the Web (Free)

This learning activity is a selected collection of free Web-based typing practice sites and tutorials on the Web. Use these to practice touch-typing and test your typing fluency. Practice is the best way to improve your typing fluency for virtual reference. There are other sites available, but these four were judged most useful for practicing typing for virtual reference. They are listed in order of usefulness, ease, and accessibility.

*   Keyboarding Practice Drills—http://www.davis.k12.ut.us/cjh/appliedtech/Business/Keyboarding/
    This site was created by Mrs. Pitcher, for teaching her business courses at Centerville Junior High School, in Farmington, Utah. She has divided keyboarding into 17 lessons with speed tests. This reminds me very much of how I originally learned to type [from Miss Harper]. Mrs. Pitcher's site links to a page with a collection of other keyboarding tests and resources: http://www.davis.k12.ut.us/district/etc/cathy/keyboarding.html.
*   Touch-Typing Exercise—http://www.sense-lang.org/typing/.
    This is also a tutorial on touch-typing basics as well as an opportunity to practice on a computer keyboard and test fluency. It can be downloaded for use offline as well.
*   TypeOnline—http://www.typeonline.co.uk/.
    Free touch-typing tutorial in five lessons, with speed test and practice. A nice feature of this site is an article on safety and exercises to prevent repetitive motion injuries.
*   Typing Exercise—http://gwydir.demon.co.uk/jo/typing/index.htm.
    This is a kind of challenge speed copy typing game. It can be a fun way to build speed and accuracy.

Learning Activity 2–2: Instant Messaging Chat Practice

This learning activity is a selected collection of links to Instant Messaging chat services that reference librarians can use for chat practice. These require that you sign up and provide some basic contact information. Once you have access to Instant Messaging you may contact me at diane.kovacs@gmail.com (GTalk), SaintsMrsDi (AOL) or diane@kovacs.com (MSN or Yahoo chat) if you would like to say hello and practice communicating with your fingers. Multi-Chat client software allows you to receive and send Internet messages on more than one IM service at a time. The IM services are listed in alphabetical order. Most of the Instant Messaging services are available for both Windows and Mac OS.

Instant Messaging Services:

- AIM (American Online Instant Messenger)—http://www.aim.com/
- GTalk (Google's Chat)—http://www.google.com/talk/ Requires a Google E-mail account. E-mail the instructor at diane.kovacs@gmail.com if you need an invitation. GTalk uses Jabber technology for IM and Voice over IP.
- Jabber—http://www.jabber.org/
- IChat—http://www.apple.com/macosx/features/ichat/
- Mac OS software uses Jabber technology for IM, Voice over IP, and other services.
- ICQ—http://www.icq.com/
- MSN Messenger /Live Messenger—http://join.msn.com/general/im-blog
- Yahoo Messenger—http://messenger.yahoo.com/

Multi-Chat Clients list can be found at http://en.wikipedia.org/wiki/Instant_messenger.

T1.2 Ability to work with multiple software applications on a computer with multiple windows, to move appropriately between windows/applications, and to move quickly and mindfully between multiple activities—chatting, searching print or electronic sources, etc. (minimal multitasking)

Observation and attention are the key components of successful multitasking.

Observe the layout and mechanisms for moving between windows and applications, as well as the options for manipulating the windows and applications.

Pay attention to which window or application you are currently "in" at any given moment. The common operating systems—Windows, Mac OS, and Linux—all have labels on any given window. In Windows, you need to be aware of your taskbar and the start menu and what is available through those tools. In Mac OS you need to be aware of your dock and how you have set it up. Linux uses similar mechanisms, depending on which desktop manager you have selected. Take the time to become familiar with your desktop and how it is organized.

Notice how to close, open, and minimize windows. Practice resizing windows. Move windows around and reorganize them on your screen to create a clear workspace.

As with most technical competencies, multitasking requires practice. Multitasking does not mean doing everything at the same time. It means doing multiple tasks in sequence. The ideal is that you do multiple tasks in logical sequence and are able to do each well. Do not try to work quickly until you can move between tasks logically and are comfortable. Speed will come with practice and experience.

Learning Activity 2–3 offers some exercises for beginning multitasking and some links to basic computer terminology glossaries. If the vocabulary used in this section does not make sense to you, you may need to take a basic computer skills workshop.

The learning activities are also available at http://www.kovacs.com/ns/ chatrefbook/chatrefbook.html.

Learning Activity 2–3: Minimal Multitasking Practice

This learning activity is a simple exercise in multitasking. Practice these basics. Add software applications of your choice. Work slowly and carefully. Build up speed gradually.

Windows XP/2000 beginning multitasking

Review the locations of the following on your computer:

1. Start menu
   o Chat software—what do you have? IM tools?
   o Web browsers—what do you have? Web Chat bookmarked?
   o E-mail software—what do you have? Web E-mail?
   o Word processing software—what do you have?
2. Task bar—monitor your Task bar and the applications that show in it as you continue with the next steps.

Multitask:

1. Open and start your Web browser, then connect to one of the following sites:
   o MetLife—Computer Glossary—http://www.metlife.com/Applications/ Corporate/WPS/CDA/PageGenerator/0,1674,P2313,00.html
   o Webpoedia—computer and Internet technology definitions—http:// www.webopedia.com/
   o The Sharpened Glossary of Internet and Computer Terms—http:// www.sharpened.net/glossary/
   o File Formats and Extensions—FileTypes Overview—http:// www.1stsitefree.com/file_types.htm
2. Open and start your word processing software.

    o Copy and paste information from one of the Web sites or the URL to a text file.

    o Save the file as text only.

    o Attach the file to your e-mail below.

3. Open/start/connect to a chat session.

    o Talk to someone on your list or connect to the instructor.

    o Copy and paste information from one of the Web sites or the URL to your chat session.

4. Open/connect to your e-mail software.

    o Address an e-mail message to someone you are chatting online to or anyone else—yourself is fine.

    o Copy and paste information from one of the Web sites or the URL to an e-mail message.

Self-reflect on this simple four software multitasking practice. How did this "feel" to you? Try adding other software applications into the practice.

Mac OSX beginning multitasking

Review the locations of the following on your computer:

1. Dock

    o Chat software—what do you have? IM tools?

    o Web browsers—what do you have? Web Chat bookmarked?

    o E-mail software—what do you have? Web E-mail?

2. Finder Window/Applications Folder

    o Chat software—what do you have? IM tools?

    o Web browsers—what do you have? Web Chat bookmarked?

    o E-mail software—what do you have? Web E-mail?

Next, repeat the same multitask steps as above under the Windows XP/2000. Self-reflect on this simple four software multi-tasking practice. How did this "feel" to you? Try adding other software applications into the practice.

T1.3 Detailed functional knowledge of how to access the Internet, use Internet e-mail, and connect to Web sites

This competency is obvious. You must know how to get onto the Internet in order to offer virtual reference service. Usually, if you work from a central location, you will be shown or given directions on how to get onto the Internet from that location. In most networked environments, this means you need a login and password that authorizes you to access the Internet through the network. Some virtual reference librarians telecommute. Telecommuters will obviously need to know how to get onto the Internet from their home or other location. Each situation will vary based on the type of connection and local arrangements for logging into a given chat reference or e-mail reference system. If you don't know, ask. Practice.

TI.4 Detailed functional knowledge of at least one Web browser

Spend some time and go from menu option to menu option in your favorite browser software and learn what each does. Click through on the "help" and read the documentation. If you know one browser well, it will make it much simpler for you to troubleshoot if something goes wrong during a virtual reference session, and you'll be able to explain or describe to users what they can do with their browser.

TI.5 Demonstrate awareness of the basic technologies that any given virtual reference service user may or may not be using, have access to, or be limited by

You cannot assume that all users have the same level of access to the Internet, or even that they have e-mail accounts, printers, fax machines, or telephones. They may be using the virtual reference service from a school or work computer that doesn't allow them to print, or that is protected by firewall software that blocks chat software co-browsing (escorting, page-pushing, application sharing), or even simple forms. The only way to find this out is to ask, try, and involve the user in troubleshooting if things go wrong. Be aware of alternatives, e.g., typing the URL for them to copy and paste into their own browser, giving detailed instructions, asking the user to "try something" then report back, and so on. Patience is key.

Your users may be connecting from dial-up or satellite access, which can be very slow or "laggy," and so they may seem to be not paying attention when the slowness is merely an artifact of the technology. Even high-speed public computer networks can become very slow during certain times of day.

TI.6 Demonstrate awareness of the chat software specifics for a given system you are going to be using

Most virtual reference librarians will go through some kind of training on the basics of the software being used. The major software you'll use for chat reference also generally provides online manuals and support. Learning Activity 2–4 tours some of the online manuals available for self-training on chat software specifics.

If you need guidance on how to evaluate and select software for virtual reference service, see Lipow (2003, Chapter 3) or Meola and Stormont (2002, Chapter 7).

The learning activities are also available at http://www.kovacs.com/ns/ chatrefbook/chatrefbook.html.

Learning Activity 2–4: Common Chat Software Overview

This learning activity is a selected collection of links to online manuals for common virtual reference software. LiveRef, Gerry McKiernan's project to compile lists of common virtual reference software and virtual reference services is also listed. Choose one of these manuals or review the manual for your own library or library organization's virtual reference software. Use the following "Virtual Reference Software Specifics to Learn" checklist as a guide to review the manual. Answer each question for your software, using the manual, or if you have access testing in the software itself.

- Internet Public Library: Ask a Question—http://www.ipl.org/div/askus/ refservice.html
- GroopZ—http://www.digi-net.com/technology/groopz/ (used by e.g, OhioLINK—http://www.ohiolink.edu)
- QuestionPoint (OCLC and the Library of Congress)—http:// www.questionpoint.org/support/ (used by e.g., Boston Library Consortium—http://www.questionpoint.org/crs/ servlet/org.oclc.home.TFSRedirect?VIRTCATEGORY=BOSTONU&SS_ COMMAND=CUST_SUP&Category=BLC
- LSSI Virtual Reference ToolKit—http://www.vrtoolkit.net/vrttour.htm (used by e.g., KnowItNow24/7—http://knowitnow.org)
- LiveRef: A Registry of Real-Time Digital Reference Services—http:// www.public.iastate.edu/~CYBERSTACKS/LiveRef.htm

Virtual reference software specifics to learn

1. How and where does the user access the virtual reference software?
   o Is access through library Web site, from any Internet Messaging client?
   o Is access primarily through a Web form or bulletin board (with or without e-mail support)?
   o Is a login and password required, or IP authentication?
   o What identifying information is required, if any (e.g, zip code, e-mail address)?
2. How and where does the user ask a reference question?
   o Type in before chat session is established or after?
   o Type in e-mail, Web form, or on bulletin board?

3. How and where does the reference librarian access the virtual reference software?
   o Is access through library Web site, from any Internet Messaging client, e-mail?
   o Is a login and password required or IP authentication?
   o Can the reference librarian work from any location with this software?
4. How and where does the reference librarian answer reference questions?
   o Directly through chat session, or Instant Messaging?
   o E-mail
   o Bulletin board monitoring and posting
5. Are there options for queuing waiting users? If so, how does the librarian manage the queue?
   o How does the reference librarian connect to a specific waiting user in the queue?
   o Can more then one reference librarian staff the same queue of users?
6. Are there options for using scripted messages? Who is allowed to create new scripted messages?
7. How are scripted messages sent to the user?
   o Automatically? Which messages?
   o Can the reference librarian select and send specific scripted messages?
8. Are there options for pushing pages to the user? How is this done? What are the limitations (e.g., specific browser required, client software required)?
9. Are there options for application sharing—co-browsing or escorting? How is this done? What are the limitations (e.g., specific browser required, client software required)?
10. What are the procedures for ending a virtual reference session? What does the software do automatically? If automatic, what scripted messages are used?
11. Are there options for post-reference session follow-up? Evaluation surveys? Can the librarian retrieve the user's e-mail address for personal reference follow-up?
12. Does the software itself offer options for information delivery (e.g., file sharing, e-mail attachments, faxing computer to computer, etc.)?

T1.6.a Detailed functional knowledge of the specific chat software used by your library or other organization for chat reference

Detailed functional knowledge is the competency level required so you can use the chat software expertly, and you can teach other people how to use it. Detailed functional knowledge of the chat software also requires that you know all of the functions of the software, those you will use routinely as well as those that might someday be useful.

Some chat software features page-pushing or application sharing, also called co-browsing or escorting. These features allow for some showing or sharing of the search process. With page-pushing, the librarian can show a site or page to a user rather than merely typing a URL to them. Application sharing allows the librarian to co-browse or escort a user through searching a Web site or database with the user, or even to share another application on her desktop with the user. Application sharing, when it works, is a marvelous tool to use during chat reference interviews. However, you cannot rely on these tools always working. Page-pushing is often blocked by the user's local firewall protection. Application sharing requires that users have downloaded and installed additional software on their own computers and that their firewall will allow the access.

This level of competency can only be achieved through direct experience and practice with the specific chat software. Receiving training will be a good start. Think about how you would teach other people to use the software. Reflect on how you learned to use the software. What worked? What did not work?

T1.7 Demonstrate awareness of how to connect to and chat through Web-based chat software, Instant Messaging, etc

To practice these skills, the best thing librarians can do is to get online and begin chatting and practicing. Learning Activity 2–2 (above) introduced some options for chatting practice using Instant Messaging software. Learning Activity 3–4 in Chapter 3 offers some options for recreational and consumer service chat practice.

T1.8 Demonstrate awareness of the options for document or information delivery

In any reference mode, we have multiple options for information delivery. The following section outlines information formats, and the technologies needed to deliver information in each format in face-to-face or virtual reference.

In face-to-face reference, all the options described in this section are usually possible for the librarian and the user. Copyright issues might still apply in regard to what may be copied and distributed under fair use, or licensing agreements may affect access of specific users to other information (e. g., Lexis/Nexis may allow downloading only by law school students).

In virtual reference, information must be deliverable in electronic format, whether scanned images of print materials (faxed or attached as files), retyped or copied-and-pasted extracts from print materials, typed or pasted citations, or downloaded or e-mail-delivered documents or search results. Downloaded or scanned materials that can be sent as e-mail attachments, or delivered via file-sharing, ftp, or Web, are desirable for ease of access for both librarian and user. However, copyright issues are not so clearly defined for the delivery of electronic copies of information. It may be advisable to refer the user to search and print or download from full-text Web-accessible databases themselves rather than for you to deliver the results to them.

Print books or journals

Face-to-face: Holding a book or journal or magazine in hand, checking them out, reading the original item.

Virtual reference: Scanning pages from print books or journals to fax, or to send as e-mail attachments, or to deliver via file-sharing, ftp, or Web.

Databases (accessible on-site only)

Face-to-face: Reading and/or printing from an on-site computer. Downloading or saving to electronic media.

Virtual reference: Printing out and scanning or faxing results. Downloading or saving to electronic media to send as e-mail attachments, or deliver via file-sharing, ftp, or Web.

Databases (Web-accessible, fee-based or free)

Face-to-face: Reading and/or printing from on-site computer. Downloading or saving to electronic media.

Virtual reference: Retyping or copying and pasting content to the chat or e-mail editor. Printing out and scanning or faxing results. Downloading or saving to electronic media to send as e-mail attachments, or deliver via file-sharing, ftp, or Web.

Full-text online books or journals

Face-to-face: Reading and/or printing from an on-site computer. Downloading or saving to electronic media.

Virtual reference: Printing out and scanning or faxing results. Downloading or saving to electronic media to send as e-mail attachments, or to deliver via file-sharing, ftp, or Web.

T1.9 Demonstrate awareness of sending files as attachments in e-mail

This process can be very simple, if you practice observation and attention. If you know that it is possible to send files as attachments in e-mail, look through your e-mail software menu options, icons, etc., to see what the mechanism is for attaching a file to a given e-mail message. Read the e-mail software help if needed.

You must always be aware of where on your computer the files you want to attach are saved or stored. That is, the path of directories, subdirectories, and the name of the file.

You might also want to find out if your local e-mail mail server blocks any particular file format. For example, my previous e-mail system used to block Web pages (.html files), and one of my colleagues has an e-mail server won't allow him to receive Word documents (.doc files). Just be aware of possible limitations and of useful alternatives. Ask users to confirm receipt of files that are important.

T1.9.a Detailed functional knowledge of sending files as attachments in e-mail

Keep in mind for yourself, your colleagues, and for your users, the fundamental safety rule of receiving e-mail attachments. Only open attached files if you expected a file from the sender. If this is a "surprise," it could be a virus or Trojan horse (see one of the basic computer terminology glossaries in Learning Activity 2–3). Take the time to contact the sender and ask if he/she sent you an attachment and, if so, what it is. The sender may be a trusted person, but viruses and Trojan horses often access address books on computers they infect and e-mail themselves to the friends and colleagues of the "trusted person." Basic practice steps for attaching files to e-mail are:

- Create a text file with a brief greeting or other professional message.
- Save the text file on your computer.
- Be aware of exactly which directory and subdirectory you are saving the file to and note the file name.
- Open your e-mail.
- Address an e-mail message to a colleague or friend.
- Type in details including the file format, the file name, the contents of the file, and the sender of the file.
- Ask the colleague or friend to confirm that they received the file.
- Attach the file to the e-mail.
- Send it.

Consider how you would explain to someone else how to attach a file in your local e-mail system. Ask a colleague or friend to send you an attached file. Observe how the file appears in the e-mail. How do you open the file? How will you explain this to a user?

T1.10 Demonstrate awareness of file transfer options (e.g., Instant Messaging, ftp, Web posting)

Depending on which chat or e-mail software you are using to offer virtual reference service, you may be able to do file transfers directly between connected users. Be aware, though, that these are frequently blocked by firewalls. Some libraries will allow you to post or upload files to a Web or ftp site to share with users. Check through your system—observe and pay attention to the menu options, icons, etc., and read the help files if any are available.

T1.10.a Ability to make use of file transfer options (e.g., Instant Messaging, ftp, Web posting)

In order to attain this advanced competency, you must be able to transfer files, or upload them to ftp or Web sites for sharing, and be able to explain to a user what you are doing. To practice, download and install an Instant Messaging client, if you do not have one already installed (see Learning Activity 2–2), and try to transfer a file to a friend or colleague. Ask about ftp or Web storage options on your local system. For example, does your library or library organization maintain an electronic reserves Web site or ftp site that you could add a document to? If so, find out the procedure for using this. Uploading files to an ftp or Web site is fairly simple once you know the local address, password, and other procedures for your ftp or Web server access.

T1.11 Demonstrate awareness of common computer file formats

Text or plain text is usually given the file extension .txt. Microsoft Word documents are .doc. Web pages are .htm or .html. Common graphics formats include .gif, .jpg, and .png. Movies might be .mpg, .ram, or .mov. Sound files could be .mp3 , .ogg, .wma, or .au. Adobe Acrobat files are always .pdf. Rich text format is .rtf. To learn about other extensions or get a more detailed sense of the formats used, use Google's Web definitions feature and type "what is .ram" (or the like) to get multiple functional definitions as well as definitions in context. At this level, you just need to know what these file extension indicate about the file itself. Can they be attached to an e-mail? Are they a format that the user can open, read, or edit?

T1.11.a Detailed functional knowledge of common computer file formats

Eventually, as you become more technically adept, you will want to locate and learn how to use applications that can edit and save files in many formats. Most computers come with a basic text editor, and most word processors allow files to be saved as plain text or .txt.

Observe and explore what you have access to and consider what your users are likely to also have access to.

Two useful sites for learning more about computer file formats are FileFormat.Info: The Digital Rosetta Stone—http://www.fileformat.info/ and The File Extension Source—http://filext.com/.

T1.12 Demonstrate awareness of the local e-mail system and limitations

The limitations of your local e-mail system may or may not be published on a shared information site, so if you don't know, ask. Limitations to be aware of include:

- size limits on messages,
- size limits on attachments,
- format limits on attachments,
- spam filters and what is done with rejected mail (i.e., is it filed where you can review it or just trashed?),
- If individual users can alter the spam filter, and
- whom to contact with technical problems or questions.

Every local e-mail system is a bit different. To learn the options available to you in a given application, review the software you are using by going through all the menu options and icons and getting a sense of the capabilities of the software. Read the help files if any are available. If you have gone carefully through all of the menu options and icons, you will have found the help files and know how to access them.

T1.12.a Detailed functional knowledge of the specific e-mail software used by your library or library organization

Detailed functional knowledge implies that you not only can use the e-mail software, but you can teach other people how to use it. Experience and practice are the beginning, but you will also want to explore features that you may not routinely use. Think about the software in terms of what could be done with it as well as what you routinely do with it.

T1.13 Demonstrate awareness of other e-mail systems and limitations

If you can, try to actually locate and look at e-mail software other than the one you commonly use. Otherwise, be aware that there are others available, and your users may be using something very different from what you are used to. Fortunately, most e-mail software shares some basic options:

- send/post e-mail messages
- receive/download e-mail messages
- create/compose/edit e-mail messages
- forward e-mail messages
- attach files

The differences will be in where in the menu each option is available, how it may be named—send might be called post or create might be compose or edit. Different graphics may be used for the icons for these options; a picture of a postal mail envelope might be used or a simple button.

You may want to get a free e-mail account on a system you've never tried before to broaden your awareness of the differences in e-mail software. Also, be aware that users may have different size limits and other factors than you have on your own local e-mail system.

T1.14 Demonstrate awareness of options to download, install, and use toolbars, search engines, plug-ins, and other helpful browser extensions

You may already have some of these installed on your Web browser depending on whether or not you are working from a computer dedicated to chat and e-mail reference. Search engine extensions or add-ons include search bars for reference tools such as WorldCat, Wikipedia, Medline Plus!, Creative Commons, and several other general search engines. Mozilla maintains a site with extensions for

Firefox—https://addons.mozilla.org/. Microsoft maintains a site for the Internet Explorer browser—http://www.ieaddons.com/.

OCLC makes the WorldCat applet available for multiple browsers through the Open WorldCat Program—http://www.oclc.org/worldcat/open/. Jon Udell's LibraryLookup bookmarklet http://weblog.infoworld.com/udell/stories/2002/12/11/librarylookup.html works with Amazon.com, BN.com, isbn.nu, and other online bookstores. When you find a book through one of these Web stores, you can use the applet to search your local library's holdings to find the book.

Most Web sites that require a browser extension that you do not have installed already will notify you that an extension is required and provide basic instructions for acquiring the extension. However, it is good to be aware of the central sources of the most common extensions in order to be able to give that information to your users. Learning Activity 2–5 offers some sites and basic instructions for downloading and installing selected common browser extensions.

The learning activities are also available at http://www.kovacs.com/ns/chatrefbook/chatrefbook.html.

Learning Activity 2–5: Useful Browser Extensions: Overview

This learning activity is a selected collection of links to brower extensions that will be useful for reference librarians with some basic instructions for downloading and installing them. The Open WorldCat browser extension is among the most useful. There are other browser extensions but these four have immediate usefulness. Not all browser extensions will work with all browsers. The central sites for Firefox and Internet Explorer are also listed. Take some time and explore what other browser extensions are available and choose those that will be immediately useful for your work. Browser extension is the umbrella term for a variety of add-on, search engine toolbars, applets, and other software that adds functionality to Web browsers.

- Open WorldCat Program—http://www.oclc.org/worldcat/open/
- LibraryLookup Bookmarklet (Jon Udell)—http://weblog.infoworld.com/udell/stories/2002/12/11/librarylookup.html
- Creative Commons (CC)—http://wiki.creativecommons.org/CcSearch
  This search engine will help you find photos, music, text, books, educational material, and more that is free to share or build upon.
- MyCroft—http://mycroft.mozdev.org/
  Browser extensions, plug-ins etc. for Firefox including Medline Plus! search, and Wikipedia search
- Microsoft Internet Explorer Add-on—http://www.ieaddons.com/
- Mozilla Firefox Add-ons—https://addons.mozilla.org/

T1.14.a Ability to download, install, and use browser extensions, and similar helper programs

Review the sites described in the basic version of this competency above and choose an extension for your favorite Web browser that you think will be useful. Browser extension download sites either walk you through the download and installation process or provide detailed instructions. I recommend that you download and practice with the WorldCat browser extension first.

Learning Activity 2–5 lists some sites where common browser extensions are located, and steps through the process of downloading and installing the Open WorldCat browser extension.

Interview Question 4

Some people will never be able to offer good chat reference service because they do not have good typing/written/synchronous communications skills either because they are not willing to learn or have other difficulties (e.g., one of my clients is a paraplegic). How would you decide if someone (or yourself) was not going to be a good chat reference librarian? Can you give an example without giving me any names or violating privacy?

KP: I had one librarian I supervised who was a fabulous librarian when it came to walk-in and phone patrons. But she could *not* do VR. She had a fundamental problem with the concept of VR—she thought that patrons "should" go out of their way to go to the library, if what they needed was all that important. That bad attitude meant that she was short and less than helpful to her online patrons. She also thought that all offline resources were poor substitutes for online ones, so she wouldn't take time to research, but would just send a Google results page.

I think that any librarian who has a problem with the whole concept of VR or with the use of online resources will never be a good VR librarian. That attitude will affect his or her ability to learn and remember the software, his or her tone when working with patrons, and the amount of research he or she will be willing to do. A VR librarian who just tells every third patron that they need to contact their local library is really doing harm to a service. I wish that only librarians who believed in and enjoyed VR could do it.

SM: Definitely people who have typing issues can be a problem because it is important to be prompt in sending messages. Delays are problematic. Also, people who are not comfortable with multitasking find chat reference overwhelming. In chat, you need to keep track of the conversation in the chat area, the Web sites the patron is looking at, the other searching you might be doing in another window. It requires a lot of components and work flows going on simultaneously. We have had some staff who opt out because they are not comfortable in this environment."

PO: I don't like to prejudge anyone's ability to do anything. I grew up with a dad who has use of only one hand and cannot walk. He was a very successful lawyer before he retired. He goes everywhere and does everything. There are many ways of achieving the communication needed for chat reference (or anything else for that matter). Some technologies merge voiceover IP with display screens. I think that good reference librarians can easily transfer the skills, and that technologies plus ingenuity overcome obstacles. We all have to do this to a greater or lesser degree. Something that really caught us unawares, though, was that many of us do not think of ourselves as young adult librarians. That age group is a big part of public library chat reference, and the background and skill of a seasoned YA librarian is really helpful in communicating effectively. Those of us who usually deal with adults or college students assume that our public will actually read a page sent, for instance, and will actually analyze the information, rather than protesting because the banner at the top says seventh grade rather than eighth grade.

JY: Some individuals will not be good e-mail reference librarians. Some librarians have a better handle on written communication skills. I think that some librarians avoid taking e-mail questions.

KLR: One of the things that software we use does is archive transcripts. As Kent State's chat coordinator, I've asked the individuals who staff chat for us to put those in a shared drive space. I plan to have the names of the staff and patron redacted and then we can review them. It allows for training and also an opportunity for peer-review without pointing fingers. In our case, however, we don't require everyone do chat reference (that is likely to change soon as we are discussing offering an IM-based service staffed by the reference librarian at our reference desk), so for now, it is self-selecting and only the folks who are comfortable are doing chat service. *KLR*

LB: Some people are just not comfortable with computers or technology. Multitasking is also difficult. I have noticed that working VR many times you have more than one question—sometimes two or three, and some in the queue. If this stresses someone out, they should not be doing VR. This is going to be a common occurrence and they must feel comfortable possibly working with more than one person at a time, switching screens, etc.

JV: I think that chat reference librarians are pretty self-selecting. Those that are comfortable or want to be comfortable generally do a good job. There are some who never get comfortable, and they know they don't like it and don't want to do it.

SH: Yes, I met a reference service provider who had majored in law.

Although willingness to learn is not an issue with him, to me, it is mostly his personality that I assume is the reason why he will not change the way he gives reference. What is amazing on this matter is that he doesn't usually receive complaints about his way of answering, probably because the students he assists (college students) don't see anything to complain about. I had the opportunity to read some of his answers, and they weren't as appropriate as they could be. I refer to the way he writes—at least to me, not very well—but the patrons' knowledge of grammar was worse, so they didn't complain if they didn't know what was wrong. Also, I think that the daily use of messaging services by the new generation of students who use chatting as a "way of speaking" has impacted the way that we see writing. It has became more common for everyone to let things go without correcting them.

T1.15 Ability to use a document scanner to scan print materials to be faxed and/or saved for transfer to the user (e.g., send as attachments by e-mail, file transfer options)

Document scanners over the past decade or so have become very simple. You need to observe or learn the following to operate one for simple image scanning:

- Where on the scanner screen do the documents need to be placed to scan the complete page?
- What software is installed on the computer to manage the scanner?
- Open the scanner software and go through the menus to learn: how to begin the scan process, how to save, and what format the image will be saved as?
- Where on the computer (which directory or folder) has the scanned image been saved?

- Can scanned images be faxed directly from the computer or will they need to be printed?
- Can the scanned image be e-mailed directly from the computer where it is stored or will you need to save it to storage media (e.g., USB/flash drive) and transfer it to another computer on the network?

References and Recommended Readings

FileFormat.Info: The Digital Rosetta Stone—http://www.fileformat.info/.

FILExt—The File Extension Source—http://filext.com/.

Hirko, Buff, and Mary B. Ross. 2004. *Virtual Reference Training: The Complete Guide to Providing Anytime Anywhere Answers*. Chicago: ALA Editions.

Lipow, Anne G. 2003. *The Virtual Reference Librarian's Handbook*. New York: Neal-Schuman.

Microsoft Internet Explorer Add-on—http://www.ieaddons.com/.

Meola, Marc, and Sam Stormont. 2002. *Starting and Operating Live Virtual Reference Services*. New York: Neal-Schuman.

Mozilla Firefox Add-ons—https://addons.mozilla.org/.

Nilsen, Kirsti 2005. "Virtual versus Face-to-Face Reference: Comparing Users' Perspectives on Visits to Physical and Virtual Reference Desks in Public and Academic Libraries." World Library and Information Congress, 71st IFLA General Conference and Council, August 14–18, 2005, Oslo. Norway. http://www.ifla.org/IV/ifla71/papers/027e-Nilsen.pdf.

Nofsinger, Mary M. 1999. "Training and Retraining Reference Professionals: Core Competencies for the 21st Century." *The Reference Librarian* 64:9–19.

Open WorldCat Program—http://www.oclc.org/worldcat/open/.

Udell, Jon. LibraryLookup bookmarklet—http://weblog.infoworld.com/udell/stories/2002/12/11/librarylookup.html

Chapter 3

Practice and Expand Communications Skills and Knowledge for the Virtual Reference Interview

With the open Web and our digital libraries as key tools, I think we hold an edge in working with the Google generation—the reference interview. I regard the reference interview as the ultimate digital killer application. Moreover, everything important about this complex dialogue can be tailored to a digital library environment. . . . At the core of the interchange lies a simple, but powerful, moment in the interview. Usually it involves the reference provider saying in a casual sort of way, "What were you really hoping to find?" At this point the hunt is on, the abstract becomes concrete, and the service provider has an opportunity to demonstrate library skill, which depends on a comprehensive, thoughtful approach to using all media, both new and historical, and both digital and print.

(Huwe, 2004: 40)

Huwe, in the article cited in the quote that begins this chapter, describes the Katharine Hepburn movie *Desk Set* (http://imdb.com/title/tt0050307/), in which a human reference department successfully competes against a machine to answer reference questions. The human advantage is in our ability to consult with our users to clarify their questions and connect new information with known information to find answers. Even the best modern "answer machines" computer software, such as Google, cannot interact with information seekers to help them frame their questions and connect effectively within variable structures of information organization and publication. Some researchers have even suggested changing the title "librarian" to "information therapist," because librarians work with users to diagnose and meet their information needs. (Huwe, 2004; Lipow, 2003)

Virtual reference service requires all of the same professional communications skills and knowledge as face-to-face reference service. The challenge is to apply, practice, imagine, and understand how to communicate professionally within the technology context described in Chapter 2 and using the reference skills and knowledge discussed in Chapter 4.

Face-to-face reference communication takes place with both the librarian and the library user being able to use nonverbal and verbal communications. Much that is obvious in face-to-face communication is not obvious in virtual communication. For example, if the librarian is sitting or standing at a desk/counter or other area with signage that designates available reference service, or walks over to where the library users are working—at a computer or in the book stacks—and offers reference service, then both know that reference service is available, and that the reference librarian is willing, able, and approachable to help the library users meet their information needs. If the user walks away with a book in hand, or begins to search and print the results, and nods when the librarian asks if his or her information needs have been met, both know the communication has been completed for the time being.

A key challenge for the virtual reference librarian is, using only text, to engage in as much of the reference communications process as possible, including making clear that willing, able, and approachable reference services are available. Virtual reference librarians must imagine and practice being welcoming and encouraging with no other communications mode except text and some consensus use of abbreviations, emoticons, and emoting (textual body language indicators).

Virtual reference service users must be aware of, value, and be able to find virtual reference assistance. The virtual reference librarian bears the burden of knowing how to locate and navigate the information resources well enough to explain to users how to do so, and why they should do so, and what they should do or will need to do with the resource in terms of searching, information delivery options, and other related factors. You can't just show them. You must be able to describe to them, in text, how to locate, navigate, and use information resources, both print and electronic. Communications competencies for virtual reference are the skills and knowledge needed to do what is done face-to-face, limited by text-only communications tools.

The communications competencies discussed in this chapter are not intended to be comprehensive. They have been selected, based on interviews with and articles by experienced virtual reference librarians and researchers, as the most essential communications skills and knowledge for virtual reference librarians. (Nofsinger, 1999; Ross, Nilsen, and Dewdney, 2002; Meola and Stormont, 2002; Lipow, 2003; Ross, 2003; Ronan, 2003a; Ronan, 2003b; Hirko and Ross, 2004; Guidelines, 2004, Nilsen, 2005, Westbrook, 2006) General reference communications competencies were introduced in Chapter 1 as well. Each competency is described in terms of learning goals—the skills and knowledge to be learned—and performance objectives—what the learner needs to be able to do with what is learned. Two of these competencies have an associated advanced level of skills and knowledge. As with Chapter 2, the advanced levels are discussed within the description of the general competency. Advice from experienced virtual reference librarians and some learning activities that might be used to practice and expand these skills and knowledge are included in the discussions. The learning activities are also available on the handbook's companion Web site.

Interview Question 5

I've identified four types of "bad" chat reference interviews:

1. The librarian reads the patron's question and does a Google search and gives them a URL without going through the interview process described above. The patron leaves the interview with a feeling that he/she already knew how to do that and what was the point?
2. The patron asks a question that requires information that is not available in the format they desire. The librarian fails to provide alternatives—e.g, referring the patron to come to the physical library to get printed sources, or to access electronic sources that are not freely available over the Web to that particular patron.
3. The librarian judges the patron based on their grammar/spelling/or subject of their question and does not work with them carefully and thoroughly or refuses to work with their subject area.
4. The patron is only using the reference service to be rude/crude/lewd or mean.

What kinds of "bad" chat interviews are you aware of? Can you give me specific examples (While respecting individual's privacy)? What "remedies" would you provide to either retrain the librarian or the patron in the above cases? e.g., #4 I would advise the librarian to cut off the interview and make a note re. possibly having them blocked from the chat service. #3 train the librarian to be aware of diversity and sensitivity to the legitimate information needs of patrons and the challenges that some patrons might experience because of literacy or physical problems. #2 train the librarians to know the reference sources: locations and licensing arrangements possible and perhaps create a Web page with those kinds of details to refer the patron to e.g., Clevnet has a list of database access information and book/serials access information. #1 See #2 :).

KP: I've had VR librarians say, "All I do is use Google to find Web sites and send them to patrons." I have told them not to feel that this is not providing a needed service to patrons. I've seen transcripts where the librarian explains to the patron that this is what he or she has done, and the patron, incredulously, replies that he or she had been trying Google for hours with no luck. Just because patrons know about tools like Google, doesn't mean they know how to use them. However, that said, I train my librarians to *never* just send a Google results list. Doing the search is only half our job—selecting the best resource(s) from a list is the other half. I look at it as the difference between saying "here is the shelf with medical books" and saying, "this book should have the information you requested."

I also encourage my librarians to follow up with patrons to make sure the resource they sent had the info the patron needed, or if they have any more questions. As I said above, I think sometimes an effective strategy is to send the patron a Web site that they librarian thinks has the info the patron needs, and then to ask, "is this what you wanted?"—sort of using a starting point to get the reference interview going.

To comment on #3—I really have never seen a transcript where I've gotten the idea that the librarian is not taking the patron's request seriously because of his or her impression of the patron based on bad spelling or grammar, or even a bad question. I'm sure it happens, both online and in person, but fortunately in my experience in public libraries (both online and in person), my colleagues have never shown disrespect for a patron because of their perception of his or her intelligence. If anything, I think librarians I've observed have been even more patient and helpful with patrons who might have trouble communicating their needs.

As far as pranks—I encourage my librarians not to take them personally. And also not to try to steer such pranksters from their evil ways—I train them just to use our suggested messages and to disconnect them. We can't block patrons from logging on, but we can note IP address and manually disconnect them."

SM: 1. In some cases, searching Google, finding the Web site, and sending the Web site to the patron is just what the patron needs. The patron leaves satisfied. So it seems the goal is to determine the extent of the information need and interest in online instruction. We work individually in order for patrons to feel they have gotten the information they need in a timely manner.

It would be worse if the librarian tells the patron that he/she can find many results by using Google and giving him/her some search terms without even performing a search. Only slightly less bad: Just sending the Google results list to the patron and asking him/her to pick and choose. Another thing that would be worse is a long description of the search process for someone who just wants the information and does not have time for instruction.

2. Another of this type of problem (which I think is worse) is when the librarian immediately instructs the patron to go to their local library and does not search or help at all. In our experience, our patrons came online to find information because for one reason or another they could not get to the library. We should do what we can to provide some online reference resources before referring to another agency. Of course, no matter the question, the librarian should always provide the information or a referral to an agency that can help. We have several special libraries and agencies and often referringl helps to promote our service as well as that of the special library. Additionally, it makes the patron feel we have provided excellent service and follow up.

3. & 4. We have found in studying transcripts of online reference that it is often challenging to determine if a patron is asking a real question or just pranking, so 3 & 4 kind of run together. We instruct staff to treat each question as a reference question and "play it straight." If the patron gets out of line, it is good to acknowledge it early and clarify what the service is and isn't. "This is a reference service. Do you have a research questions?" "Diane, I am happy to help you with research, but if you continue to be rude, you will be disconnected." We have found that when librarians ignore chat that is goofy or slightly rude, the patron's rudeness escalates. If we call them on it early, they often turn around. We have also found in studies of our transcripts that people who are goofing around or rude can be turned around and the reference transaction can be successful. We consider every transaction an opportunity to inform the patron on what the service is, how to use the service as well as to help them with their information.

Other obviously bad reference transaction techniques:

Librarian misunderstands the question and sends information that does not relate to the reference need. For example, "I need photographs of posters from WWI" and the librarian sends images of posters from WWII.

Librarian does not ask enough questions to understand the reference need and sends unrelated information. This happens often online because of this feeling that we need to provide information quickly. Ironically, it can end of taking more time in the end because of the miscommunication.

Patron introduces tangents and the librarian and reference process gets derailed. This can be tricky because we don't want to seem unfriendly when asked if we like donuts or how old we are. However, we need to steer the patron back to the task at hand.

PO: The above are true. Sad to say, though, the librarian often looks bad in spite of everything because the patron has visited the service at a time when it is too busy, or because they need more instruction in use of a resource than they have time for, or because the patron has unrealistic expectations of the speed or scope of the service they want.

Badly behaving patrons can be a real trial. We have canned messages to say their language in inappropriate, etc. The canned messages are great because they prevent us from using our fast typing skills to tell them what they really deserve to read! Some staff are willing to put up with a lot and jolly these people along until they (sometimes) decide to use the service appropriately. Others among us cut them off pretty fast. We don't take abuse in person, and there is no reason for that online either. It does seem that some patrons lose all social graces when they go online.

All of the ideas (solutions to "bad" chat) above are good if sensitivity training is backed up by access to some resources. Problem has been for statewide service, that the resources or needs tend to be very local. A Cleveland librarian may be aware of services in that area, but have difficulty serving a patron located elsewhere in the state. For licensing agreements, OPLIN has done a good job of making a set of databases available statewide.

JY: I have never been specifically instructed to be aware of sensitivity and diversity in the e-mail reference arena beyond the sensitivity we should already be using during in-person desk reference interviews. I am sure there is room to enlighten chat and e-mail responders about how certain words and phrases in print might appear derogatory, condescending or subject to misinterpretation.

KLR: The biggest problem I've run into is confusion about what OhioLINK Chat is. Since it is a consortial service staffed by librarians of member institutions, we frequently get students who do not realize that the librarian they are chatting with is likely not from their own school. So they ask really specific questions that only someone at their institution can deal with (like questions about library fines or about the construction going on in front of the library at another school at the opposite end of the state). Example #1 is by no means limited to chat reference—that happens all the time at the reference desk too. It is a matter of training. I almost always ask where the patron has looked already—and more importantly, *how* they were searching. There is a teachable moment there—if the patron is willing to cooperate and isn't in an all-fire hurry. Same for #2—this is a training issue—and needs to be addressed whether the transaction is chat or in person. However, it is also possible that the lack of referral is because the *patron* only wants online sources—I've had that happen even at the reference desk where I've told them the article is available in our periodicals collection but because it wasn't full-text online, they didn't want it. You have to be responsive to them—if they only want one thing, then telling them something else is pretty much point-less (plus, since we deal with students, a good portion of the time they are on a deadline and can only use stuff they can get their hands on immediately).

#3 is troubling—the negative reaction to someone's grammar or typing just seems so unlikely—if a person is reacting that way, they definitely should be in a different profession (it seems like they'd do that when dealing with in-person ques-tions as well). The part about refusal to help with a subject I tend to regard as an acknowledgment by that individual that they may not be *able* (rather than willing) to help a patron with that topic. Referral is a common aspect of in-person ser-vice; it is much trickier to pull off in a chat situation. On OhioLINK Chat, we can refer to a librarian from the patron's home institution—and sometimes we need to do that if the question is specific to that library or a resource that they have that we do not.

#4—this isn't something I've run into—which may be because I staff an aca-demic service rather than a public library service. I'm sure it does happen, I just haven't experienced it. The suggestion of banning someone though may not work—on OhioLINK's software it is not uncommon for the patron to be anonymous—they don't have to give a name or e-mail address. Frequently they are sitting in their home library, so it makes it really difficult to ban someone if you don't know who they are.

LB: One of the most difficult situations online I have encountered several times is someone (you think a junior high or high school student) says they are doing a paper on a sexual or controversial topic. You never know if this is going to be someone playing a joke, or someone legitimately asking a question. I have had the question, "How are babies born?" I tried to ask if it was for a paper—sometimes it takes several questions to tell if it is a joke or not. Sometimes students take you on a merry ride to see how far you will go, and other times you find out immediately it is a joke and an abuse of the service.

One thing I've just realized is that when I starting doing/supervising/teaching VR 5 years ago, I focused on what made it different from traditional reference. Now, I see more similarities than differences. In training, we often meet librarians who are very concerned about how to handle certain issues—"What if the pa-tron swears at me?" "What if I'm busy with another call?" "What if I can't find what they want?" And we say, "What would you do if the patron was in person or on the phone?" And it's funny and satisfying to see the librarians process that for a second, and then relax: "Oh yeah, I've been handling that for years.

JV: From my experience reading transcripts, we definitely have problems with #2– 4. With #2 our bigger problem, I think, is convincing a patron that they need to come in in-person because the answer to their question is actually in a book. Sometimes a patron will log in and ask the same question to 2 or 3 different people before he/she is convinced of the need to come to the library in person. I think the best you can do is try to offer a couple of different options and hope that will do the trick. We definitely have some trouble with #3. First-year college students are not going to pay attention to grammar, spelling, etc., and some of them are very bright! This has been hard to overcome but I think we've made good headway. It's important to just repeat, over and over, that spelling, grammar, punctuation, etc. just don't matter much in a chat environment. We get #4 all the time. We just end the session, tag as "inappropriate," and move on. Sometimes we get patrons who aren't inappropriate but who seem to be looking for social contact rather than reference help. We have to end those sessions too, sometimes quite firmly. But that happens in-person in libraries all the time.

SH: In our library is like this: the first sources to be searched must be a) the ones that library owns and b) the ones that patron can reach more easily.

We only use Internet sources on specific occasions: 1. As the last resource. 2. When we know that only this information can be find there and no one else have it 3. When we are not sure of the subject and try to clarify it (this #3 is not for giving it to patrons, just for ourselves).

As you probably know Virtual University is part of the ITESM System, and because the majority of our students are located around the globe (mostly our country) a big percentage of them enter through one of the campuses located in Mexico. Those students are able to use the material in the libraries of each campus (even more, they have all the services that each campus offers to regular students) but it is consider independent from our service. However, we (librarians) are in contact all the time to avoid conflicts of interests among our policies and in our special case, we are responsible of the good service that the physical library will give to our patrons.

This particular situations allow us to recommend physical material that belongs to any library on campus and to offer interlibrary loans with external institutions that some campuses have to their regular patrons. For example: Campus Monterrey has more than 15 interlibrary loans arrangements with national and international libraries; we, aware of this, can send our patrons to use this service with confidence, whether or not we are part of the arrangement. Of course, I consider it my responsibility to know about those arrangements in order to use it in my answers to the patrons.

I think that reference service providers that have been working on this, for long time, learn that sometimes we ignore many terms or subjects that any— *any*—patron would ask at any moment, so I would recommend to be humble and place ourselves in the teacher role but also, carefully guide patrons to learn the correct way (of grammar, spelling or subject) in a subtle manner. This is something that nobody can teach you but it is important to be aware of.

This rude, crude kind of patron can be ignored as much as we choose. The best part of being in a virtual position is that they will never be able to see our faces, and it will depend on us to not fall into the game.

I have an example that could be "failure" reference, and it happened to me. After that, I learned how to answer better to patrons who need closer assistance.

To begin, I must say that one of our policies in reference service consists of *not* providing the exact answer to the patron but giving him clues to find it or teaching how to "create" a strategy. So, this person asked: "I need two or three articles about technologies in education." Then I mentioned which databases she could use and how to develop a search strategy to find them. Then she replied that her expectation was to receive the articles through this service. Then I explained to her using, more or less, these words:

"We do not send all the articles we find because there are too many results, and it is necessary that you decide which ones will be better for your research. That's why it is more convenient guiding you to tell you 'how' to find them in the different databases in order to let you analyze them and choose the ones more appropriate for your research."

The patron obviously got angry and told me she had already looked in other sources, that she understood better, and now she knows that our service does not provide documents like she thought.

Now I know, that I should probably give her some of the results I found (so she will know there was information) and ask her which kind of trouble she had using the database.

Believe me, I learned the lesson!!"

Communications Skills and Knowledge for Virtual Reference Librarians:

- C1.1 Ability and awareness of the need to continue learning technical, communications, and reference skills and knowledge
- C1.2 Awareness and understanding of good reference interviewing skills and techniques for virtual reference service
  - o C1.2.a Detailed functional knowledge of good reference interviewing skills and techniques

- C1.3 Ability to empathize with virtual reference users during a virtual reference interview, and to understand something of the culture and social environment of the Internet
- C1.4 Ability to explain library and research processes without using library jargon
- C1.5 Demonstrate awareness of the need to imagine and project a professional persona as part of library participation in the Internet community—"library space" on the Web
- C1.6 Ability to provide information without making value judgments, to maintain and project professional objectivity
- C1.7 Ability to carefully and quickly read and respond to the text typed by a library user and displayed on a computer monitor—communicating to the user that you are "listening"
- C1.8 Understanding of the need and the ability to "be there" for the virtual reference user—avoiding "silence"
- C1.9 Understanding of when and how to teach or instruct during a virtual reference transaction
- C1.10 Demonstrate awareness of when and how to provide follow-up, referrals, or to request consultations with other professionals
- C1.11 Ability to work with multiple users in a virtual reference only environment
  - o C1.11.a. Ability to work with multiple users in a mixed virtual reference and face-to-face environment
- C1.12 Detailed functional knowledge of typing quickly and fluently on a computer keyboard in order to communicate—typing fluency

C1.1 Ability and awareness of the need to continue learning technical, communications, and reference skills and knowledge

To be a librarian is to be a lifelong, continuous learner. In order to be a good virtual reference librarian, you must make it part of your ongoing routine to maintain, supplement, and add to your technical, communications, and reference skills and knowledge. Virtual reference librarianship is not going to be a viable career option for individuals who cannot adapt as the information industry, the technical infrastructure, and social dynamics change. In *Libraries in Science Fiction*—http://www.ku.edu/~sfcenter/library.htm—James Gunn explores some of the fascinating, strange, amazing, and sometimes prescient ways that libraries, librarians and library services have been imagined by science fiction writers. It is reassuring to realize how many science fiction writers assume that we librarians and libraries will be present in future and alternate universes, albeit in diverse forms, providing extraordinary services to our users.

C1.2 Awareness and understanding of good reference interviewing skills and techniques for virtual reference service

Good reference interviewing skills and techniques as discussed in Chapter 1 are important regardless of the communications mode through which reference service is offered. Learning Activity 3–1 offers some excellent free Web-based training for an introduction to good reference interviewing skills. Practice, experience, observation of skilled virtual reference librarians, and attention to the specific challenges of chat and e-mail communication are the most effective training strategies for virtual reference librarians.

The learning activities are also available at http://www.kovacs.com/ns/ chatrefbook/chatrefbook.html.

Learning Activity 3–1: Web-based Tutorials for Good Reference Interviewing

This learning activity is a selected collection of links to Web-based reference interview tutorials and virtual reference transcripts to use for learning or reviewing reference interview skills. Visit one or more and go through the tutorials and related learning resources to review and reinforce your reference interviewing skills.

- Ohio Reference Exellence (ORE)—http://www.olc.org/ore/1intro.htm
- DREI Digital Reference Education Initiative—http://drei.syr.edu/
  Many reports, articles, shared experiences, tutorials, etc. on this site.
- Digital Reference Education Inititiative (DREI) Digital Reference Transcripts— http://128.230.185.43/item_list.cfm?NavID=22
- InfoPeople "Reference Interview Skills"—http://www.infopeople.org/training/ past/2004/reference/
- Introduction to Reference123. Houston Area Library System—http:// www.hals.lib.tx.us/ref123/1intro.html
- The Reference Interview—http://web.utk.edu/~wrobinso/ 590ref_interview.html

C1.2.a Detailed functional knowledge of good reference interviewing skills and techniques

Practice, experience, observation of other reference librarians at work, reading professional articles that reflect on the needed skills and attitudes, and report research are all needed to attain detailed functional knowledge of good reference interviewing skills and techniques.

The competencies that follow are all directly related to the foundation competency of being able to conduct a good virtual reference interview. Keep in mind that, even in virtual reference, the good old advice is still relevant:

> The path to success is a calm Zen-like attitude. This is based as much upon a good disposition as confidence in when to say, ever so politely "Let's see what we can find." Work in a reference area will point the way. Reference sources inevitably will disclose answers to even the most remote, difficult query. And if not a precise response, at least it will be a reply which will satisfy.
>
> (Katz, 2001: 25)

C1.3 Ability to empathize with virtual reference users during a virtual reference interview, and to understand something of the culture and social environment of the Internet

Some of those who are most negative or critical about virtual reference services (Coffman and Arrett, 2004a; Coffman and Arrett 2004b, and McKinzie, 2002) point out the difficulties of establishing a relationship with users through text-based communications tools. This difficulty is not a reason to reject virtual reference. By identifying the difficulty, we can develop strategies to overcome the problem. We can develop good professional relationships with our users through virtual reference. In order to do so, we must not only be able to type fluently but we must be able to "be there" for our users and to behave as though they are "real." Recognition of the existence of a fellow human being however remote is key. To be able to do that requires some understanding of the culture and social environments of the Internet.

Society Online: The Internet in Context (2004) and *The Internet in Everyday Life* (2002) are collections of essays and research reports about who Internet users are in real-life and how they act, project personas, and participate in social interactions as part of the Internet community. Griswold and Wright (2004), for example, report research that indicates that Internet users are also readers. Although they do not make the connection to Internet users also being library users, readers do tend to be library users. Haythornthwaite and Kazmer (2002) discuss the need for distance library school students to be aware of the real-world existence of their fellow students and teachers in order to have a positive learning experience supported by virtual communications and in a school community on the Internet. Their research was specifically with library school students, but their findings apply to librarians working online as well:

> Students will feel alone when online if they have not gone beyond the communication with the computer and reached instead communications with others through the computer... they move from a stressful position of isolation to confident membership in the online world.
>
> (Haythornthwaite and Kazmer, 2002:456)

Use your imagination to visualize the real-life existence of the virtual reference user. Keep in the forefront of your mind that you are interacting with another human being through the text interface.

Ronan (2003a:46) thinks that "In some ways chat encourages better reference interviewing..." Ford (2003) reports that her research shows the need for the virtual reference librarian to make "creative use" of all of the textual communications options available in order to make-up for the lack of nonverbal cues from the user during the interview. Westbrook (2006:254) includes an "Establishing the Information Need and User's Affective State" step before beginning to analyze the question. In essence, it is important for the virtual reference librarian to ask the user to provide details or to pay attention to any details volunteered that convey information about the urgency of the information need, the user's comfort level with the technology, and other states of mind that might affect the interview process. Buckley (2006) advises that we pay attention particularly to statements made in virtual reference that convey the user's state of mind or emotion especially if that state of mind is uncomfortable, anxious, unhappy, worried etc.

> Such situations call for an extra dose of empathy and understanding... You should not try to judge, but instead put yourself in their place and consider what you would like in that situation.
>
> (Buckley, 2006:132–133)

C1.4 Ability to explain library and research processes without using library jargon

Did you use the word monograph in a sentence today? Librarians, as do other professionals such as doctors, lawyers, and teachers, use technical terms or jargon to speak amongst themselves. There are two good reasons for using simple and plain language to explain library and research processes to virtual reference service users:

1. Keeping the chat or e-mail communication as clear and concise as possible
2. Ensuring that users understand the guidance we are giving them and can make use of it

Compare a doctor telling a patient "you have idiopathic hypertension" with a reference librarian telling a user "you need to consult a bibliographic database." Both use jargon that is meaningless to most nonprofessionals. The first we can look up in a medical dictionary and find, according to the Merriam-Webster medical dictionary, at http://www.nlm.nih.gov/medlineplus/mplusdictionary.html, that the doctor is telling the patient he has unexplained high blood pressure. In the second case, of course, the librarian is telling the user to search for journal articles and possibly books and book chapters using a computer search tool. "Idiopathic hypertension" is a scary diagnosis; "bibliographic database" can be just as scary to nonlibrarians. Saying what is meant in plain language allows patients or users to get directly to solving their problem.

When providing reference services, you need to remember that you are not speaking to our fellow librarians, nor do you need or want to train reference service users to be librarians. The librarian vocabulary may be confusing for many current, as well as potential, library users. John Kupersmith has published "Library Terms That Users Understand"—http://www.jkup.net/terms.html—based on user studies of terminology used on library Web sites. His intention is to provide usability data as well as "best practices" on which terms "most users can understand . . . well enough to make productive choices . . . " of library resources and services. It may make sense to librarians to refer to bibliographic databases but users find "Search Electronic Journals" or "Research by Subject" more understandable.

C1.5 Demonstrate awareness of the need to imagine and project a professional persona as part of library participation in the Internet community—"library space" on the Web

Virtual reference librarians need to create a library Web culture, a "library space" that is part of the Internet community, where they can act as librarians on the Internet. It is the librarian's role, the librarian's persona. You are not chatting or e-mailing for recreation, or for scholarly or collegial purposes. You are acting as an information professional. This can be very challenging. In order to "be there" for users, you need to project a persona through textual interactions in chat and e-mail. Your word choices, grammar, and style of interaction all affect how others perceive the librarian's professional persona in virtual communications.

In her chapter in *Society Online*, Eszter Hargittai (2004) discusses how people using the Web, especially for information seeking, are more successful, and more likely to become better searchers, if they know who and where to turn for assistance. Although she is reporting data collected about personal networks of support, her findings are very relevant to librarians.

> . . . people may be discouraged by the difficulties of finding information on the Web and so may end up spending less time with the medium, resulting in continued lower level skills. Moreover, those who can draw on family and friends for advice have continuing support to help their online skills or, at least, to alleviate some of the frustrations caused by confused Web searching . . . People rely on their social support networks for suggestions of site recommendations and for answer to particular questions that come up as they look to the Web for answers to questions. . . .
>
> (Hargittai, 2004:271)

Librarians and libraries should be part of that social support network on the Web, as they are part of that social support network in the face-to-face communities they serve.

Lorri Mon (2006) interviewed e-mail and chat reference users on their perception of virtual reference service for her dissertation research. She found that users preferred personal responses, such as librarians sharing their names and addressing users by name, and that they spoke negatively about impersonal "form letter" responses. Users also positively mentioned librarian uses of many of the interaction techniques recommended in the ALA/RUSA behavioral guidelines for information professionals.

The professional librarian persona requires being a bit more formal than the user, but not stiff or rude. Conversational interactions should be more informal than a lecture but more formal than just chatting with friends. Do not be tempted to use chat slang or "be one of the kids"; they want us to be librarians and that is why they have connected to the chat or e-mail reference service. Virtual reference service users expect us to be literate and to type in full sentences, but not be baffled if they use abbreviations or emoticons. (Personal and professional communications; Squire and Steinkuehler, 2005) This does not mean your grammar and spelling must be perfect. Abigail Rovner (2005) reviewed transcripts for instances of "chat speak"—abbreviations, emoticons, emoting, and spelling/capitalizing shortcuts—during virtual reference interviews as well as the virtual reference literature. Her findings were that the use of these conventions does not cause communications problems as long as both the reference librarian and the user understand conventions. Misspelling, deliberately abbreviating, or failing to properly capitalize titles, author names, and other citation information does cause problems. Informal conversational styles of communicating worked well as long as the critical information was spelled correctly and properly communicated.

Conversational style rather than scholarly publication style is always preferable for clear communications. Spelling is critical for titles, author names, URLs, and other citation information, but obsession with correct spelling and grammar should not be allowed to slow down the reference interview. Do your best and remember you can always retype to correct. One common convention is to retype a misspelled word with an asterisk in front. So if I typed "deliberatley abreviated," I can retype on a new line "*deliberately *abbreviated." Librarians need to know what users mean if they use abbreviations or emoticons, but can't assume that all virtual reference users understand the common abbreviations and emoticons. If the user first makes use of these communications devices then you can also use them, since it has been established that the user knows what they mean. (See the Common Chat and E-mail Abbreviations, Emoticons, and Emoting list below.)

Using Learning Activity 3–2 as a guide, you can practice virtual reference role-playing to get a sense of "persona" as well as the process of reading and responding in typed text. Learning Activity 3–3 is a guide for e-mail reference practice and observation opportunities.

Virtual reference interviews may take more time than in-person interviews because we have to tell each user who we are and what we can do for them, and must type rather than speak or act.

The learning activities are also available at http://www.kovacs.com/ns/chatrefbook/chatrefbook.html.

Learning Activity 3–2: Practice and Observe Chat Reference

This learning activity is a role-play and observation.

You are the chat reference service user. You will be observing your own and a virtual reference librarian's responses and actions. You may connect to a real virtual reference service and ask a reference question. Or you may ask a colleague to play the virtual reference librarian while you ask a reference question using Internet messaging. This is learning activity is based partially on Hirko and Ross's "Secret Patron" activity (2004:57)

1. Choose one of the reference questions from the list provided in the "Optional Reference Questions to Use for Learning Activities 3–2 and 3–2" table below. *or* Write down a question or questions of your own. If you cannot decide, try asking, "I need to know about asparagus." This will give you a wide scope for testing the reference interviewing skills of the chat reference service. Decide what your backstory will be: backyard gardener needing planting information, agriculture scientist needing latest hybrid research, cook needing recipes, etc.

2. Decide if you will be a secret patron or if you will ask the virtual reference librarian if he or she has time to role-play with you, and ask them questions about the process as you work with them. You may also choose to work with

a colleague known to you through IM or local chat reference software.

3. Connect to the chat reference service that serves your academic or public library community. If you do not know if your library offers chat reference check for it in the sites: LiveRef: A Registry of Real-Time Digital Reference Services—http://www.public.iastate.edu/~CYBERSTACKS/LiveRef.htm—or the Collaborative Live Reference Services. Bernie Sloan—http://people.lis.uiuc.edu/~b-sloan/collab.htm

4. Ask your question. Identify yourself if appropriate. Self-reflect: how does the librarian interview you as a user? Does the librarian elicit the pertinent details of your information need? If you are identifying yourself, does the librarian respond positively? Does the librarian let you know if the service is too busy to accommodate your questions? If you are a secret patron, do you have to wait long for a response? How does the librarian handle your question initially? Canned message? Does the librarian identify him or her self?

5. Self-Reflect: What type of information do you, the user, need? Known Item or General Information? What type of question was asked? Directions, policies, ready-reference, specific-search, research?

6. What does the virtual reference librarian ask you or otherwise respond? Does the librarian conduct a reference interview? That is, does the librarian attempt to determine your real question? Is the librarian approachable? Does the librarian show interest? How? Does the librarian explain or otherwise share a search strategy with you?

7. What will you, the user, do or say in response to the virtual reference librarian? How is the reference interview concluded?

8. Other things to consider for real-life practice that you do not need to respond to for optional role-play activity:
   • How do you, the user, indicate that you are dissatisfied or satisfied with the response to your question?
   • Consider the impression—attitude, intelligence, etc.—you think you convey as a virtual reference user.
   • Describe the reference person's attitude (e.g., friendly, forthcoming, reluctant, irritable, short, etc.). How do you "know"?
   • What are your impressions or feelings? Describe what you noticed.

9. Turnabout: Ask a colleague or friend to role-play and IM or Web chat with you as a user asking a question. You role-play the part of the virtual reference librarian. Ask your colleague to critique your reference interview skills, etc.

Learning Activity 3–3: Practice and Observe E-mail Reference

This learning activity is a role-play and observation.

You are the e-mail reference service user. You will be observing your own and a virtual reference librarian's responses and actions. You may connect to a real virtual reference service and ask a reference question. Or you may ask a colleague to play the virtual reference librarian while you ask a reference question using Internet Messaging. This is learning activity is based partially on Hirko and Ross's "Secret Patron" activity (2004:57)

1. Choose one of the reference questions from the list provided in the "Optional Reference Questions to Use for Learning Activities 3–2 and 3–3" table below. *or* Write down a question or questions of your own. If you cannot decide, you might ask "What information do you have on Art?" This will give you a wide scope for testing the reference interviewing skills of the e-mail reference service. Decide your backstory: Art history science question— looking for water colors and when people started using them. Art learning how to paint with water colors. Art chemistry: what is the chemical make-up of water color paints? Toxicology? Be a student, hobbyist, medical student, or parent concerned about a child.

2. Decide if you will be a secret user or if you will ask the virtual reference librarian if they have time to role-play with you and ask them questions about the process as you work with them. You may also choose to work with a colleague known to you through your local e-mail reference software.

3. Connect to the e-mail reference service that serves your academic or public library community or ask a question on a public e-mail reference service such as Internet Public Library: Ask a Question—http://www.ipl.org/div/askus/.

4. Ask your question. Identify yourself if appropriate. Self-reflect: how does the librarian interview you as a user? Does the librarian elicit the pertinent details of your information need? If you are identifying yourself, does the librarian respond positively? Do you have to wait long for a response? How does the librarian handle your question initially? Canned message? Does the librarian identify him or her self?

5. Self-Reflect: What type of information do you, the user, need? Known Item or General Information? What type of question was asked? Directions, policies, ready-reference, specific-search, research?

6. What does the virtual reference librarian ask you or otherwise respond? Does the librarian conduct a reference interview? That is, does the librarian attempt to determine your real question? Is the librarian approachable? Does the librarian show interest? How? Does the librarian explain or otherwise share a search strategy with you?

7. What will you, the user, do or say in response to the virtual reference librarian? How is the reference interview concluded?
8. Other things to consider for real-life practice that you do not need to respond to for optional role-play activity:
   - How do you, the user, indicate that you are dissatisfied or satisfied with the response to your question?
   - Consider the impression—attitude, intelligence, etc.—you think you convey as a virtual reference user.
   - Describe the reference person's attitude (e.g., friendly, forthcoming, reluctant, irritable, short, etc.). How do you "know"?
   - What are you impressions or feelings? Describe what you noticed.
9. Turnabout: Ask a colleague or friend to role-play and e-mail with you as a user asking a question. You role-play the part of the virtual reference librarian. Ask your colleague to critique your reference interview skills, etc. You might consider volunteering on the IPL e-mail reference service http://www.ipl.org/div/askus/ service as additional real-life experience and practice as a virtual reference librarian.

Optional reference questions to Use for Learning Activities 3–2.

NOTE: You may also write down questions of your own to use for these activities. These are real-life questions that have been preresearched so we know approximately what kind of answers/information will be found. Consider your backstory. Use your imagination and experience to act as a realistic user.

Consumer Health

A general practitioner believes that a female patient might have cluster headaches. Where can the patient find a report on headache diagnosis and treatment?
   A patient has heard that it is not necessary to perform a hysterectomy to remove uterine leiomyomas (fibroids). Where can she find information on the surgical or drug treatment of uterine leiomyomas on the Internet?
   Do you have any medical books?
   I need information about Multiple Sclerosis?
   Do you have a book about herbal cures?
   How can I find out if my doctor is a quack?
   I need a book about how to tell if you're pregnant—for my friend.
   How do I tell if my baby has lead poisoning (or arsenic, or other poison).
   Do you have a book on Alzheimer's?

Genealogy

A genealogical researcher needs to know if she can get vital statistics for her state/county/country/province (pick a state/county/country/province of your choice) on the Internet, or can she order them through the Internet?

Can you find a census index, transcription, or scanned image for your state/county/country/province? (pick a state/county/country/province of your choice)

I need to find my grandfather's death certificate.

Do you have any books on <surname>?

Do you have any books on finding adoptive parents?

My family came from this county, this little book says you have the census records here at the library.

My grandfather was a revolutionary war hero. Do you have a book about him? (or Civil War, or WWII, or WWI).

My mother says the library is scanning in her diary and newspapers records. Where do you keep them?

Do you have the address of the Ohio Historical Society?

Legal

Do you have any divorce forms? (or adoption, or lease, or bankruptcy)

Do I need a lawyer if I want to sue my neighbor for damages?

How do I incorporate?

What are the custody laws between New York and Ohio?

I need to know how to legally change my name (or adopt my spouses' children or grandchildren)

Do you have a list of DUI lawyers?

How old do you have to be to drive a truck? a big-rig. (or limo, or taxi, or other commercial transprot)

Business

Your mom, who wants to run her own quilt shop, needs information on small business loans and planning assistance. Where can she find them on the Internet?

I'm applying for jobs at several different companies. I have interviews with Sherwin Williams, American Electric Power, and Timken. How can I find them on the Web so I can learn more about each company in preparation for my interviews?

Do you have company history for The J.M. Smucker Co.? (or any other company)

How do I know if my business is required to pay sales taxes?

Do you have any books on investing?

I need a list of addresses for all of the companies in x county in x state. (use a county and state of your choice)

I read on the Internet that I can get free grants for my business here.

Who owns Proctor and Gamble? (or any other company)

Do you have books about doing business in other countries? (choose a country)

Children's Questions

In my high school speech class we have to find speeches by two different people and compare and contrast them. I've been assigned: Thomas Jefferson's "Commerce between Master and Slave", and Frederick Douglass' "What to the Slave is the Fourth of July?" The library reserves doesn't have any more copies of the speeches I need. Where can I get copies on the Internet?

A teacher has assigned the history and rememberance of the Holocaust in her 6th and 7th grade Modern History class. What supporting resources for her students can you find on the Internet? What resources can you find that would talk about critical thinking in studying history? (e.g., historical revisionists)?

Who is the inventor of the first automatic traffic light (3rd grader)

What was the name of that guy who really wrote Shakespeare's plays? (high school)

What does "warm-blooded" mean? (6th-grader)

I need pictures of the Rock (or any other celebrity who interests children ages 6–18). Fill in the celebrity you've heard of or been asked about most often by children you work with or know.

I need a book on how to win the Science Fair (8th-grader)

How do you spell circumnavigate? (4th-grader)

Why is Columbus the capital of Ohio? (7th-grader)

Readers Advisory

Would I like Isaac Asimov's children's stories? (6th-grader)

What is Danielle Steele's real name?

I read this book where five kids go to Europe. It was an old book. Do you have it? It was something like Salt or Pepper?

Who is that writer who writes all those mystery stories about an archaelogist in Egypt in the 1800s? The best character is named Peabody I think.

The newspaper said that there is a new book out about Alaska do you have it?

What does it mean when this book says its a "Caldecott Medal" winner? (or "Newbery Honor" winner)

Do you have any books about how to get a teenager to abstain from premarital—you know, activities?

C1.6 Ability to provide information without making value judgments, to maintain and project professional objectivity

Maintaining professional objectivity can be easier if we also maintain a sense of humor.

It is a failure of reference service if a reference librarian judges a user based on the subject of their question and refuses to work with them. It is also a failure of reference service when virtual reference users are judged on their grammar and spelling and the virtual reference librarian does not work with them carefully and thoroughly as a result of that judgment.

Enemark (2006) reports on research projects (Epley and Kruger, 2005; Kruger, Epley, Parker, and Ng, 2005) in which e-mail receivers' judgment of e-mail correspondents' intelligence was almost always incorrect when based on factors such as the grammar and spelling. Other parts of the research indicated that when the e-mail receivers had prejudged their correspondents based on incorrect assumptions about their intelligence, the subsequent conversation was flawed.

The librarian must help the user to feel comfortable in coming to the librarian for help by using welcoming language, inviting the user to ask a reference question, and offering to provide assistance.

Greet the user by typing "How may I help you?" or "My name is Di and I'm a reference librarian, how may I help you?" Don't just start answering the user's question even if a chat software auto-response has already sent you their question. If the chat software auto-response sent you the question, then something like "My name is Di, and I'm a reference librarian, your question is X" and copy and paste their question or paraphrase their question. Then begin with a reference interview query to begin analyzing their question as appropriate—"What aspect of x interests you most?" or "I don't want to duplicate your own searching, can you tell me what sources you've already tried to find this information?" Think about how you would feel if a doctor just looked at you without speaking and then wrote you a prescription and left the room.

Be sympathetic if they express anxiety in using the virtual reference service. Be honest. Share some reassuring information. For example, if you are a slow typist, or if they use an abbreviation you don't understand—tell them. Remember, the user also might be a slow typist, or their connection might be dial-up, so be patient with their responses. Don't assume slowness means rudeness, or that a short delay means they have disconnected. Check with them—"Is everything working okay for you?" or "Are you still with me?"

Some users will present reference interview problems that might challenge our ability to maintain professional objectivity. For example, they:

- may not be willing to share the specific information required to address their questions successfully;
- may not have the specific information needed to answer their questions successfully;
- may share sensitive personal, family, medical, legal, or other information that may or may not be needed to answer their question; or
- may be unhappy if they perceive that the librarian is uncomfortable with their question or unwilling to assist them.

Here are some ideas for handling virtual reference interview problems:

If the user is not willing to share the specific information required to address their questions successfully

A calm and pleasant response from the librarian to the user is essential. It may be possible to gently reassure them that their information will be kept confidential and that you will not be judgmental. Type something like: "Without X information, it will be more difficult to answer your question, but I can give you some sources that might be helpful." Tell them about or send them the sources that you think are most likely to help them and that are accessible for them to search themselves. Offer to provide searching instruction. For example, one user I worked with asked, "I need a death certificate for my grandfather." I asked her for her grandfather's first and last name, and where he had lived at the time of his death. She replied that she just wanted me to tell her how to get death records. She was clearly reluctant to tell me her grandfather's name. I did not push the issue in any way. I sent her the URL and basic instructions for accessing the Social Security Death Records (SSDI) database through RootsWeb http://www.rootsweb.com and the Vital Records Web site http://www.vitalrec.com. I offered to explain how to search these sources, but she responded that she didn't require any instruction.

If the user does not have the specific information needed to answer their questions successfully

If the user simply does not have specific information needed to address their question successfully, then back up and work on finding that information first. For example, one user asked for "a true story of the history of Hypatia, the first librarian." The librarian found several books, articles, and Web sites on the history of libraries, Hypatia, and the Library of Alexandria (including http://en.wikipedia.org/wiki/Hypatia). None were satisfactory to the user. The librarian then asked the user if he could provide more specific information about what he needed to do with the information about Hypatia. This query elicited the information that this was for a college world history class for extra credit assignment. The librarian asked the user to type the assignment wording into the chat session. The extra credit was being given for reading an historical novel about the Hypatia who was the First Librarian. Either of two titles were included in the professor's reading list. Both titles were available; however, the user was not a student of the university who's reference service he had contacted. The librarian connected to the student's college's library catalog and found that both titles had been placed on reserve for the course.

Always offer constructive options. For example, a user I worked with through e-mail wanted to know if her great-grandfather had come from Ireland. Her father's and grandfather's last name was Regan. Both were named William. She did not know her great-grandfather's first name but thought it might have been Patrick, and his last name might have been O'Regan. She also did not know when he might have come to the United States. A search of the Ellis Island Records database http:// www.ellisisland.org retrieved more than a hundred Patrick Regans and a more manageable number of Patrick O'Regans. In order to discern which of these immigrants might be her great-grandfather, more data was needed. Our conclusion was that she needed to obtain her grandfather's death and birth certificates from appropriate agencies and hope that those records contained given and surnames, and some dates that might be used to get an approximate idea of which of the entries in the Ellis Island Records might be that of her ancestor.

If a user shares sensitive personal, family, medical, legal, or other information that may or may not be needed to answer their question

Some users just want to chat. This has been the case in face-to-face reference services and continues in virtual reference as well. Many librarians enjoy conversing with users. However, there are times when the reference service is too busy to spend much time in socializing. Simple courtesy in asking the user to come back when the service is less busy is usually all that is needed. In chat, it can be more difficult, but be sure to remain courteous and use text to redirect the user to their original reference question or the sources you have recommended or will recommend. Use concluding language, "If you need additional assistance come back later"

If the information being shared is very personal or is making you uncomfortable, the situation may be more difficult to manage. This is the time when the "calm Zen-like attitude" can help. A courteous redirection of the user to their actual information needs may suffice.

Medical information, especially when related to sexual issues, can be especially difficult to handle. Librarians may be overly sympathetic to medical problems or we may be overly embarrassed by certain topics. Siegel (2006) reviewed the literature pertaining to librarian attitudes about sex and sexuality and how they impact reference service, and then conducted his own survey. He found that librarians tend to be relatively comfortable with these topics, but he felt there was a need to train librarians in handling these kinds of questions. It can be difficult to know if a user is asking a legitimate question or is attempting to be rude. To offer the best service we must assume each question is legitimate until and if other information from the interaction indicates otherwise.

If it is clear that the user is being rude, then cut the connection. You do not have to tolerate dirty chatters anymore than you would tolerate flashers or dirty phone callers. If they are just flirting, you may find it is more positive to clarify that you are a virtual reference service and not a dating service. (Braxton, 2005) In a library service context, you may find that handling nonthreatening chat flirts positively will result in them using the library in a positive and appropriate manner in the future.

Be careful not to give advice. Reiterate that you can help them find information on their topic but they may need to consult with a medical, legal, or other professional; offer to help them locate an appropriate referral.

Be careful not to be judgmental. For example, one user asked for the Ohio Revised Code (ORC) sections on child support enforcement. While I searched the ORC (http://onlinedocs.andersonpublishing.com/oh/lpExt.dll?f=templates&fn=main-h.htm&cp=PORC), he insisted on sharing with me that he had successfully fathered 18 children and he could give my husband some advice. I redirected the interview by asking what additional information the user needed, if any, once we had located the Ohio Revised Code sections covering enforcement of child support payments. He needed the contact information for his county prosecutor's office as well.

Users may also be sharing family medical and legal details that are essential for successfully answering their question. On one occasion in e-mail reference, a user asked for books on the genetic diseases associated with brother-and-sister marriages. My first e-mailed response was to send her a citation for a medical text available in the library and offer to locate the phone number and address of a genetic counselor. Subsequent e-mail interaction uncovered the fact that she was working on a mystery book in which a murder motivation related to a genetic outcome of a brother-sister marriage played a major role in the plot. Given that additional information, I searched PubMed for articles that gave the kind of detail she actually required and e-mailed her a search-set.

If a user is unhappy, or if they perceive that the librarian is uncomfortable with their question or unwilling to assist them

Despite our best efforts, some users will never be happy unless we give them a level of service that is only available in science fiction novels, e. g., brain-to-brain information transfer, as in Neuromancer (Gibson, 1986) or a holographic personal on-call librarian avatar, as in *Snow Crash*. (Stephenson, 1993)

Sometimes users may feel that we are unwilling to assist them, especially if the librarian has reminded the user that we can only help locate information for them, we cannot solve their problem. The only thing we can do is to be as open as possible. Restate that you are a librarian and can help find information but that a medical, legal, or other professional might be able to provide better advice or assistance. It can be very hard to be nonjudgmental in some situations. Sometimes silence is the best policy—or redirection.

Occasionally, users will be upset about the results of their research, especially if the answers do not support their belief about some medical, legal, historical, or business situation. Users may also be philosophical about the research results or may dismiss the information as being "incomplete" or not accurate in some way. A nonjudgmental response can keep the situation from becoming unpleasant. Never say "I told you so" or insist to the user that the information is accurate and they are wrong. In the case of a medical or legal question, you may want to advise that they consult with a medical or legal professional.

C1.7 Ability to carefully and quickly read and respond to the text typed by a library user and displayed on a computer monitor—communicating to the user that you are "listening"

Virtual reference users cannot see you paying attention or "listening" to them. It is important to remember to acknowledge all responses, even if only by typing "okay" or "hmmm" or a smiley face. Query to be sure you understand the question. Restate or paraphrase what you think they mean and ask if that is what they mean. Use of the pre-scripted options in specific chat software is sometimes an option, but the core skills are facility with reading and typing, as opposed to the face-to-face core skills of being articulate speakers and verbal listeners.

Ross, Nilsen, and Dewdney (2003), supported by years of in-depth research, have identified four common problems in reference service that relate directly to the librarian's failure to listen to the user. These same problems can occur in virtual reference.

1. The "without speaking she began to type maneuver"—the librarian silently begins to search without giving any acknowledgment or explanation

This is a huge problem on the Internet, where users cannot see us working, and have no idea whether we are even aware of their presence unless we type a response. Hirko and Ross (2004) report that some of their students who were observing chat reference services found this a common problem in chat software that allowed page-pushing or co-browsing. They would suddenly find a page popping up and they had no idea why it was there, or even in some cases how to get back to the chat window. It is important to explain to the user that you are going to send them a page, or that you are going to open a new window and you should both be able to see what happens during a search. This preparation is very important if the page-pushing or co-browsing runs into technical limitations. For example, many firewalls block both.

2. Bypassing the reference interview—giving an answer without checking what the real question is

In chat reference, it is very easy to copy and paste or retype—rephrase—the question and get clarification. That acknowledgment also reassures the user that you understand their question, that you are listening.

3. Systems-based perspective—using language that the user does not understand, acronyms, tool names, librarianese, assuming they know how the library is structured

In chat reference, it is even more important to try to either be jargon-free or to verify that the user understands what you are saying. Don't make the user struggle. Even the most experienced library user may not be fluent in our jargon. Users rely on librarians to mediate between them, the information technology, and the information itself.

4. Unmonitored referral—sending someone elsewhere without offering alternatives, clear information about why they are being referred, and options for re-contacting

These are the kinds of librarians whom Professor Deb Johnson once called the "pointer sisters" (class lecture UIUC GSLIS 1989). They can't be bothered to search for the users' real information need or to take the time to reassure the user that the referral will be the answer. In chat reference it is very important to reassure the user, make sure you type in detail where you are referring them, and receive confirmation of understanding if possible.

C1.8 Understanding of the need and the ability to "be there" for the virtual reference user—avoiding "silence"

Face-to-face reference librarians need to "show interest." Face the user, listen to the user, respond to questions, talk with the person as you search, call attention to resources you are sharing, and so on. Showing interest through chat means typing responses, using language where you would use body language—e.g., type "/me nods" or "*nods*" in some chat software, or making conversational comments regarding what you are doing or the connection speed. Carefully reading and re-stating the question also "demonstrates an interest in the problem a well as a commitment to solving it. Sometimes simply stating the question triggers a clarification that is part of the search process for the patron." (Westbrook, 2006:254) Buckley (2006:132) also discusses the importance of the virtual reference librarian retyping the question back to the user during virtual reference: " . . . to display interest and make sure they are really hearing what the patron is communicating."

Let the user know that the search they want may require a given amount of time as well, especially if a print source is needed and/or scanning or faxing. Explain to the user what you will be doing to answer their question if it will take time, or if you will have to 'go away' for a time: "Sorry this is taking some time" or "This will take a couple of minutes—do you have time to wait?" Don't be afraid to ask them to search a Web-accessible source while you are working on something else.

Project a presence, and make sure that you are "staying in touch" during virtual reference transactions. And always verify user understanding.

Always communicate—type—to users while using page-pushing, co-browsing, escorting etc. Otherwise they have no idea what you are doing or plan to do.

The most important virtual reference communications strategy is to keep communicating, keep telling users what you are doing and telling them how to proceed. We cannot always show them or see exactly what they are seeing, but we can type questions, comments, instructions, or status queries as we work together so they know we are "there."

Learning Activity 3–4 explores recreational and consumer services chat to use in gaining a deeper understanding of social interactions that take place through Web communications.

The learning activities are also available at http://www.kovacs.com/ns/chatrefbook/chatrefbook.html.

Learning Activity 3–4: Recreational and Consumer Services Web Chat Practice

This learning activity is a selected collection of links to recreational or consumer services chat sites that the author has personal experience with. These are relatively "safe" and friendly sites. Choose at least one of each type and connect. Self-reflect. How do you feel chatting for fun? Do you feel comfortable with a particular group? How do you feel as a customer inquiring with a consumer services chat?

- Meta Chats: The Internet Chat Resource Guide—http://www.ibiblio.org/ dbarberi/links/chats/
  Collection of Web chats of all sorts.
- Gaia-Online—http://www.gaiaonline.com/
  Free role-playing game and chat intended for children primarily. Recommended to me by 7-, 10-, and 12-year-old neighbor girls. Chat and user forums are moderated actively.
- Carnage-Blender—http://www.carnageblender.com
  This is a free strategy game, with moderated chat. No cursing/swearwords are tolerated. Note that most chat is game-related. Warning: may be addictive. Author's husband is an administrator and she is a former administrator for this game.
- LandsEndLive—http://www.landsend.com
  Click on "customer service" on the main page to connect to LandsEndLive. While shopping on this site you can connect to a customer service representative to ask questions about color, quality, fabrics, sizes, etc. The author has used this for matching on-sale items to get a second opinion on matching/ combining colors and styles. This is not meant as a commercial endorsement but only an option for chat practice. You may choose to connect and just tell them you are curious about the chat option and how it works. If you wish to do so, ask the customer service representative whether he or she likes working this way?, are there problems?, etc.
- TurboTax Online Live Chat—http://turbotax.com
  Click on "Support" on the main page. Then look for "Online Live Chat." While using the TurboTax software you can connect to a tax advisor and get real-person advice. The author has not used this personally but it seems like a potentially good idea. Connect to ask about the software and service for 2006 taxes. This is not meant as a commercial endorsement but only an option for chat practice. You may choose to connect and just tell them you are curious about the chat option and how it works. If you wish to do so, ask the customer service representative whether he or she likes working this way?, are there problems?, etc.

C1.9 Understanding of when and how to teach or instruct during a virtual reference transaction

Virtual reference librarians should be aware of and prepared to search available information sources, but should offer and be prepared to explain how to locate a given information source and how to search it. If the user does not want to be taught and just wants the librarian to do the search and retrieve the information, then you can reassure the user that you will continue to be "present" while you are doing the search. Sometimes the user just wants the librarian to provide "an answer."

In many academic libraries, it is policy to offer instruction rather than just giving answers. Sometimes users need instruction in research methods or how to perform a search in a given reference source. When in doubt, ask users if they would like you to explain how to do the search. Include users in the search strategy. Ask them to search some reference source while you search another one, and then exchange notes. Work together. Use technology for co-browsing if it is available. With typing fluency and the ability to give clear instructions, chat is a great tool for teaching searching and research skills. It is possible to search together in real time—even if your chat software does not allow co-browsing—as long as you communicate consistently and clearly with the user.

Giving good instruction in text can be very challenging. It is even more challenging if you have to do so in situations where users are not be able to "see" what you are describing unless they follow along with you. A useful strategy is to type the instructions as though you were speaking them. Remember to type specific directions, such as which key to press, or which specific elements to pay attention to.

Woodard and Arp (2005) have compiled an excellent literature review of articles related to the philosophy of reference service that emphasizes teaching individuals to find information themselves over merely providing the answer—or at least explaining to the user what you are doing in the virtual reference situation.

Staff need not only to know how to apply reference interview skills in the online environment, but they also need training in how to ask questions that get at student's prior knowledge, challenge their assumptions about information and research, and help them think critically about research. They need to see their role in questioning, challenging, suggesting, diagnosing, troubleshooting, and facilitating.

(Woodard and Arp, 2005: 203)

C1.10 Demonstrate awareness of when and how to provide follow-up, referrals, or to request consultations with other professionals

The ability to conduct a good reference interview in chat reference makes it a great way to answer many reference questions. But, some questions require more time and concentration than the librarian can dedicate while staffing chat reference. Offering to get back to the user with more information via e-mail—or even telephone—is a good follow-up strategy. Most users of virtual reference will have e-mail. For those users who do not have e-mail or do not want to share their e-mail address, a phone number might be used; or you could ask them to come to the physical library so you can help them more directly.

Consult appropriately with other librarians or affiliated services through chat, telephone, or other means. But make sure the user knows what you are doing. If you are making a referral, explain why and to whom and give complete contact information. Remind them they can come back again and again to get clarification and further assistance, or if the referral was not effective.

How do you know when the reference interview is concluded satisfactorily? When does it end? In face-to-face reference, the end of the interview might be noted when the user walks away from the desk. However, it is a good practice to always ask the user if their question has been answered or if they have enough information to get started. Always offer that they can return to the virtual reference service or to face-to-face services for additional assistance.

What if you cannot answer the question or provide the needed sources? Referral to alternative sources, other professionals, other libraries, special libraries are all possible. Be honest. If you don't have the information accessible for a given user, or if you just don't know what to do to assist them, tell them. Offer alternatives with as much detail as possible, and also make sure the user knows they can return to you for additional ideas if the referral fails.

Catherine Pellegrino (2004) reviewed transcripts of chat reference interviews for her Master of Science in Library Science paper with the hypothesis: "that, in the virtual environment, reference interviews where the librarian asked open questions were more likely to end successfully than those where the librarian did not ask open questions." She found that in her sample of chat reference transcripts, open-ended questioning was not necessarily the best predictor of successful reference outcomes. She did find some very interesting results. There were no really unsuccessful outcomes in her sample. This was because the librarians were able to give good and appropriate referrals:

> Even in cases where the librarian was completely unable to provide the information the patron was looking for, patrons nevertheless consistently

thanked their librarians. It is also important to note that in virtually all cases where the librarian was unable to find the specific information the patron was looking for, he or she provided a referral or suggested an alternative for the patron: for example, giving the patron the phone number for the reserve desk when a reserve reading wasn't available, providing the URL for an InterLibrary Loan request form when a journal article was not available in the NCSU collection . . .

(Pellegrino, 2004)

Learning Activity 3–5 guides you to professional discussions with your colleagues on the Web on many virtual reference related topics.

The learning activities are also available at http://www.kovacs.com/ns/chatrefbook/chatrefbook.html.

Learning Activity 3–5: Participate in Professional Discussion Lists and Blogs for Virtual Reference Librarians

This learning activity is a selected collection of professional discussion lists and blogs for virtual reference librarians. Subscribe to at least one discussion list and monitor at least one blog. As additional virtual reference blogs and discussion lists are identified they will be added to the book Web site.

Some e-mail discussion lists are:

- DIG_REF
  Discussion of digital reference/virtual reference services
  Archives: http://groups.yahoo.com/group/dig_ref/
  Subscribe: Send email to LISTSERV@LISTSERV.SYR.EDU with the message:
  SUBSCRIBE DIG_REF Your-first-name Your-last-name
  Contact: Joann Wasik jmwasik@ericir.syr.edu, Blythe Bennett
  blythe@ericir.syr.edu, Jeremy Morgan richlist@ericir.syr.edu
- ERIL-L
  Discussion of electronic resource issues, especially for electronic resource librarians.
  Archives: http://listserv.binghamton.edu/archives/eril-l.html
  Subscribe: Send e-mail to listserv@listserv.binghamton.edu with the message:
  subscribe ERIL-L YourFirstName YourLastName
  Contact: Abigail Bordeaux, bordeaux@binghamton.edu or ERIL-L-request@LISTSERV.BINGHAMTON.EDU
- LiveReference
  Discussion of live reference services.

Subscribe: http://groups.yahoo.com/group/LiveReference/
Contacts: Bernie Sloan, Lori Bell, et al. livereference-owner@yahoogroups.com
- Libref-L
  Discussion of library reference concepts, issues and service.
  Archives: http://listserv.kent.edu/archives/libref-l.html
  Subscribe: Send e-mail to listserv@listserv.kent.edu with the message:
  subscribe Libref-L YourFirstName YourLastName
  Contact: Diane K. Kovacs diane@kovacs.com
- PUBLIB
  Discussion of issues relating to public librarianship. "Particularly appropriate
  issues for discussion on PUBLIB include, but are not limited to: Collection
  development, acquisitions, management and weeding, including traditional and
  new media Reference services"
  Archives: http://sunsite.berkeley.edu/PubLib/archive.html
  Subscribe: Send the message "subscribe PUBLIB YourFirstName
  YourLastName" to listserv@sunsite.berkeley.edu
  Contact: Sara Weissman weissman@main.morris.org or
  Karen Schneider kgs@bluehighways.com
- Web4Lib
  Discussion of the practical use and philosophical issues of the World Wide
  Web in library contexts.
  Archives: http://lists.webjunction.org/wjlists/web4lib/
  Subscribe: http://lists.webjunction.org/mailman/listinfo/web4lib
  Contact: Roy Tennant roy.tennant@ucop.edu or Thomas Dowling
  tdowling@ohiolink.edu.
- Note: Many virtual reference consortia and software discussion groups exist.
  Membership is restricted to consortia members or librarians at libraries using
  specific virtual reference software. Inquire with your consortia or software
  company/organization.

Some useful blogs are:

- Virtual Reference Blog—http://askalibrarian.wordpress.com/
  From their site: "Virtual Reference is a space for librarians and library staff to
  talk about chat, instant messaging, email and other online reference services.
  Virtual Reference is hosted by the Virtual Reference Committee of the
  Machine Assisted Reference Section (MARS)/Reference Services Section (RSS)
  of the Reference and User Services Association of the American Library
  Association. If you would like to join us at conferences or become a virtual
  committee member, contact Joe Thompson, jthompso@bcpl.net or Jana

Ronan, jronan@ufl.edu."

- The Shifted Librarian—http://theshiftedlibrarian.com/
  Jenny Levine's blog about critical library technology, especially reference and communications related.
- TametheWeb—http://tametheweb.com/
  Michael Stephen's blog about teaching library technologies, much about reference and communications
- LibDex—Library Weblogs—http://www.libdex.com/weblogs.html
  Index of Web logs relating to librianship and information specialists.

C1.11 Ability to work with multiple users in a virtual reference only environment

This requires experience and practice, but it is not much different than what librarians have been doing all along in managing multiple users at a physical reference desk. Face-to-face, you can make eye contact, but in virtual reference you must make some kind of simple text reassurance that you will be with the user as soon as you are able; prescripted messages in chat software or e-mail can be a good fallback. The virtual reference librarian needs to be aware of the user waiting for service, through the queue provided by the chat software or listing in e-mail, and to serve each person in turn. If the queue becomes too long, as it might at the physical reference desk, you should be able to call in assistance from other librarians. Don't panic. Chat seems to be immediate, and especially if you are using Internet Messaging software that has sound effects, it may seem as though many people are clamoring for attention all at once. Messages or status statements that make clear your status with other users and the potential for you getting to their question in a timely way can ensure that users do not become impatient or unhappy, so long as the messages are used consistently and frequently.

Interview Question 6

What is the most important factor you know of in giving chat reference librarians the professional confidence to be effective? Is there anything else you'd like to share?

SM: Our reference librarians tell me they think online chat reference is fun. They like the challenge of the online questions and the variety of interactions. They feel it helps build their skills in working on the library reference desk as well.

Our librarians tend to feel a pressure to provide information more quickly in the online environment. I think this expectation is kind of interesting and can be seen both on the patron and the librarian sides. I encourage staff to remember that chat reference is not instantaneous (average of 12–15 minutes for general questions and 20–23 minutes for college research). I encourage them within the chat transaction to explain this process to the patron. Naturally, when we can find the exact thing in a few minutes, it does wow the patron. However, while we have them on the line, we can explain the service to the patron in a bit more detail (rather than posting some long explanation on a Web site that nobody reads). Often when the customer gets this individual attention (and their information), they appreciate the service even more.

PO: I think librarians will really enjoy the ability to supply information in more depth by sending it to the screen. This is much more effective than talking on the phone or looking over someone's shoulder.

JY: Librarians develop experience and confidence with every reference interview and the same holds true for the online reference. Practice is an important factor. Maybe just as important would be to read your answers twice before sending them off—typos from the library are extremely embarrassing due to people's expectation that librarians have a command of the language.

A fifth phase of e-mail reference, all reference really, is the very important follow-up. Not an unsolicited note—rather ending every communication as you would on the reference desk with, "Have I answered your question?"

KLR: Just to remember that the skills you use in answering questions at the reference desk still work, though the medium is very different. The key is that the other person typing needs your help—and it's your job to help them—just like at the desk."

LB: I have found practice and mentoring so the librarian feels comfortable is the most important factor—knowing when it is appropriate to forward a question."

C1.11.a Ability to work with multiple users in a mixed virtual reference and face-to-face environment

This is not that much different than what reference librarians do every day in a busy reference center or at a busy reference desk. Librarians must manage queues of users in-person and on the telephone. Some virtual reference services are staffed by the same reference librarians who are at the same time, staffing the face-to-face reference desk. This can be managed efficiently if two or more reference librarians are working together and can trade off monitoring the two modes of reference service. One person trying to do both may have to deal with times when one queue or the other will be relatively busy. Library policy should establish which queue has precedence. Many libraries have an in-person user priority policy. The main challenge is to make sure that the in-person users know that you are also working on the virtual reference service and to let the virtual reference users know that you are staffing in-person as well. Don't panic. The worst thing that can happen is that someone gives up and goes away. If you can ask them to wait, or come back later, you've already made the situation that much better. Communicating clearly and honestly is the key.

C1.12 Detailed functional knowledge of typing quickly and fluently on a computer keyboard in order to communicate—typing fluency (See also Chapter 2, Technology Skills and Knowledge)

Kara L. Robinson, one of the OhioLINK chat reference librarians, reminds us that "chat moves a LOT faster—and if you take too long to formulate a response, they could be gone before you finish." (Instant message)

In writing about chatting for virtual reference, I almost feel like great-grandma, talking about my first Model-T and how it compares to the zippy little Ford Focus I drive today. Back in the days of BITNET (http://en.wikipedia.org/wiki/Bitnet), when I was an undergraduate and then in library school, we chatted using PLATO (http://en.wikipedia.org/wiki/PLATO) and Bitnet Relay Chat (http://en.wikipedia.org/wiki/Bitnet_Relay_Chat, specifically UMNews/CSNews), then an early form of Internet Relay Chat (http://en.wikipedia.org/wiki/Internet_Relay_Chat), and then MUDs, and MOOs (http://en.wikipedia.org/wiki/MOO). By the time I began my first professional position, the Cleveland Free-Net chat (http://en.wikipedia.org/wiki/Free-Net) was thriving and beginning experiments in chat-based medical information service (through Case Western Reserve University Medical School students).

It was an easy switch for me to move from chatting recreationally to chatting professionally. In 1994, I began using chat for teaching Web-based courses for librarians and library paraprofessionals through Diversity University MOO (sadly, now defunct). Now when I teach using chat, I can type as fast as I can talk—almost.

Chat reference requires reference librarians to be able to type to communicate. Fluency is desirable. The only way of becoming fluent in any communication mode is to practice. Chatting recreationally will be time well-spent developing fluency for professional chat reference service.

Common Chat and E-mail Abbreviations, Emoticons, and Emoting

Abbreviations (see also http://en.wikipedia.org/wiki/List_of_Internet_slang_phrases)

1337—"leet" (from "elite") "leetspeak" slang mix of numbers and letters used as shorthand by some recreational chatters/gamers (http://en.wikipedia.org/wiki/Leet)
afaik—as far as I know
afk—away from the keyboard
asl—age sex location—used to initiate flirting
brb—be right back
bf—boyfriend
gf—girlfriend
heh—short laugh-like response
lol—laughing out loud
np—no problem
omg—oh my gosh*
rofl—rolling on the floor laughing
rtfm—read the fat* manual
tyvm—thank you very much
ty—thank you
yw—you're welcome
     *Less offensive term substituted for explanatory purpose

Emoticons (see also http://en.wikipedia.org/wiki/Emoticons)

:)—regular smile
;)—winking smile
:D—big smile with teeth
:P—smile with tongue sticking out
:')—tongue-in-cheek smile

8)—either smile with glasses or goggle-eyed smile
:(—sad
:'(—crying

Emoting (textual body language indicators)

/me nods or *nods*
/me hugs or *hugs*
/me smiles or *smiles*
/me shrugs or *shrugs*
<g> or <grins>

> Note "/me" in some chat software is a command that changes the text to an action statement. For example, in the chat software I currently use in teaching LEEP courses, "/me nods" becomes "Dikovacs nods."

References and Recommended Readings

Braxton, S. 2005. "On My Mind: Eeewww! My Patron Tried to Pick Me Up." *American Libraries* 36 no. 4:30.

Buckley, Chad E. 2006. "Golden Rule Reference: Face-to-Face and Virtual." *The Reference Librarian* 93:129–136.

Coffman, Steve, and Linda Arret. 2004a. "To Chat Or Not to Chat: Taking Another Look at Virtual Reference." *Searcher* 12 no. 8 (September):49–57.

Coffman, Steve, and Linda Arret. 2004b. "To Chat Or Not to Chat: Taking Another Look at Virtual Reference." *Searcher* 12 no. 7 (July/August):38–47.

Digital Reference Education Inititiative (DREI) Digital Reference Transcripts—http://128.230.185.43/item_list.cfm?NavID=22.

Enemark, D. 2006. "It's all About Me: Why e-mails are so easily misunderstood. *Christian Science Monitor* May 15, 2006. Web edition http://www.csmonitor.com/2006/0515/p13s01-stct.html.

Epley, N., and J. Kruger. 2005. "When What you Type Isn't What they Read: The Perseverance of Stereotypes and Expectancies over E-Mail." *Journal of Experimental Social Psychology* 41 no. 4:414–422.

Ford, Charlotte. 2003. "An Exploration of the Differences between Face-to-Face and Computer-Mediated Reference Interactions." Ph.D. Dissertation, Indiana University, School of Library and Information Science. Advisor: Stephen Harter.

Gibson, William. 1986. *Neuromancer.* New York: Ace Books.

Google Answers: Researcher Training Manual—https://answers.google.com/answers/researchertraining.html

Griswold, W., and N. Wright. 2004. "Wired and Well Read." In *Society Online: The Internet in Context.* Eds. Howard, P. N., and S. Jones, 203–222. Thousand Oaks, Calif.: Sage.

Guidelines for Behavioral Performance of Reference and Information Service Providers. 2004. Reference and User Services Association, American Library Association. http://www.ala.org/al/Arus/Arusaprotools/referenceguide/guidelinesbehavioral.htm.

Gunn James. *Libraries in Science Fiction.* http://www.ku.edu/~sfcenter/library.htm.

Hargittai, Eszter. 2004. "Informed Web Surfing: The Social Context of User Sophistication." In Howard, P. N., and S. Jones (eds.). *Society Online: The Internet in Context.* Thousand Oaks, Calif.: Sage Publications: 257–274.

Haythornthwaite, C., and M. M. Kazmer. 2002. "Bringing the Internet Home: Adult Distance Learners and Their Internet, Home, and Work Worlds." In Wellman, B., and C. Haythornthwaite (eds.). *The Internet in Everyday Life.* Oxford, England: Blackwell:431–463.

Hirko, Buff, and Mary B. Ross. 2004. *Virtual Reference Training: The Complete Guide to Providing Anytime Anywhere Answers.* Chicago: ALA Editions.

Howard, P. N., and S. Jones (eds.). 2004. *Society Online: The Internet in Context.* Thousand Oaks, Calif.: Sage Publications.

Huwe, T. 2004. "Being Organic Gives Reference Librarians the Edge over Computers." *Computers in Libraries* 24 no. 5(May):39–41.

InfoPeople "Reference Interview Skills"—http://www.infopeople.org/training/past/2004/reference/.

Internet Public Library: Ask a Question—http://www.ipl.org/div/askus/.

Introduction to Reference123. Houston Area Library System—http://www.hals.lib.tx.us/ref123/1intro.html.

Katz, William A. 2002. *Introduction to Reference Work, Volume I.* 8th ed. Columbus, Ohio: McGraw-Hill.

Kruger, J.; N. Epley; J. Parker; and Z.W. Ng. 2005. "Egocentrism Over E-Mail: Can We Communicate as Well as We Think?" *Journal of Personality and Social Psychology* 89 no. 6:925–936.

Kupersmith, John. "Library Terms that Users Understand" www.jkup.net/terms.html.

Lankes, R. David; Joseph Janes; Linda C. Smith; and Christina M. Finneran (eds). 2004. *Virtual Reference Experience: Integrating Theory Into Practice.* New York: Neal-Schuman.

Lipow, Anne G. 2003. *The Virtual Reference Librarian's Handbook.* New York: Neal-Schuman.

McKinzie, Steve. 2002. "Virtual Reference: Overrated, Inflated, and Not Even Real." *The Charleston Advisor* 4 no. 2 (October):1–3.

Meola, Marc, and Sam Stormont. 2002. *Starting and Operating Live Virtual Reference Services.* New York: Neal-Schuman.

Meta Chats: The Internet Chat Resource Guide—http://www.ibiblio.org/dbarberi/links/chats/.

Mon, Lorri, and Joseph W. Janes. 2004. "The Thank You Study: User Satisfaction with Digital Reference Service." 2003 OCLC/ALISE research grant report published electronically by OCLC Research—http://www.oclc.org/research/grants/reports/janes/jj2004.pdf.

Mon, Lorri. 2006. User Perceptions of Digital Reference Services. Ph.D. Dissertation, University of Washington, School of Information. Advisor: Joseph W. Janes.

Nilsen, Kirsti. 2005. "Virtual versus Face-to-Face Reference: Comparing Users' Perspectives on Visits to Physical and Virtual Reference Desks in Public and Academic Libraries." World Library and Information Congress, 71st IFLA General Conference and Council, August 14–18, 2005, Oslo. Norway—www.ifla.org/IV/ifla71/papers/027e-Nilsen.pdf.

Nofsinger, Mary M. 1999. "Training and Retraining Reference Professionals: Core Competencies for the 21st Century." *The Reference Librarian* 64: 9–19.

Ohio Reference Exellence (ORE)—http://www.olc.org/ore/1intro.htm.

Pellegrino, Catherine A. 2004. Reference Interview Strategies in Virtual ("Chat") Reference: Effect of Open Questions. Master of Science in Library Science Paper, University of North Carolina at Chapel Hill, School of Information and Library Science. Advisor: David Carr—http://etd.ils.unc.edu/dspace/bitstream/1901/26/1/catherinepellegrino.pdf.

QuestionBoard—http://web.library.uiuc.edu/ugl/qb/.

The Reference Interview—http://web.utk.edu/~wrobinso/590ref_interview.html.

Ronan, Jana S. 2003a. "The Reference Interview Online." *Reference & User Services Quarterly* 43 no. 1 (Fall):43–47.

Ronan, Jana S. 2003b. *Chat Reference: A Guide to Live Virtual Reference Services*. Westport, Conn.: Libraries Unlimited.

Ross, Mary B. 2003. "Secret Patrons and Virtual Field Trips: The Sequel." *CLENNExchange* 19 no. 3: 1–3.

Ross, Mary B., and Daria Cal. 2002–2006. "Anytime, Anywhere, Answers: Building Skills for Virtual Reference." http://vrstrain.spl.org/.

Rovner, Abigail J. 2005. Chat Reference and Chat Speak. A Master's Paper for the M.S. in L.S degree, School of Information and Library Science of the University of North Carolina at Chapel Hill. Advisor: David Carr.

Ross, Catherine Sheldrick , Kirsti Nilsen, and Patricia Dewdney. 2002. *Conducting the Reference Interview: A How-To-Do-It Manual for Librarians*. New York: Neal-Schuman.

Ross, Catherine Sheldrick. 2003. "The Reference Interview: Why it Needs to be Used in Every (Well Almost Every) Reference Transaction." *Reference & User Services Quarterly* 43 no. 1 (Fall):37–43.

Siegel, J. 2006. "Let's Talk About Sex(uality): The Librarian's Response." Paper for LBSC 762.

Social Security Death Records (SSDI) database through RootsWeb—http://www.rootsweb.com.

Squire, K., and C. Steinkuehler. 2005. "Meet the Gamers." *Library Journal* 130 no. 7:38.

Stephenson, Neal. 1993. *Snow Crash*. New York: Bantam Spectra.

Vital Records Web site—http://www.vitalrec.com.

Westbrook, Lynn. 2006. "Virtual Reference Training: The Second Generation." *College & Research Libraries* 67 no. 3 (May):249–59.

Woodward, Beth S., and Lori Arp. 2005. "One-on-One Instruction." *Reference and User Services Quarterly* 44 no. 3 (Spring):203–209.

Chapter 4

Maintain and Build Reference Skills and Knowledge

Virtual reference librarianship is dependent upon many of the skills required of conventional reference librarianship, including: the ability to conduct an effective reference interview, to communicate effectively, and to cheerfully assist the user in selecting and using the best resources. If a VR librarian does not have those basic skills, one librarian in the survey stated, "no matter how good the technology is, it won't make up for an ineffective reference librarian."

(Lindbloom, Yackle, Burhans, Peters, and Bell, 2006:6)

Can good communications competency make up for poor reference competency? Can great reference competency balance poor communications competency? How far does being nice, approachable, listening, or always positive get you if you cannot meet or answer the information needs of your library users? How far can having thorough reference knowledge get you if you can't communicate your knowledge to the information seekers who will benefit from it?

Both communications and reference competencies are important. Without good communications skills a librarian will have a difficult time being a good reference librarian. However, without solid competence in reference skills and knowledge, a librarian is not a librarian.

This reference expertise is why information seekers—all potential and current library users—will choose to use virtual reference services instead of just Googling on their own.

In order to be successful, virtual reference librarians must also have the technical competencies discussed in Chapter 2 and be able to practice the communications competencies discussed in Chapter 3.

Reference competencies involve searching, critical thinking, and information organization skills, as well as knowledge of specific reference sources and information-finding tools. Competent reference librarians are aware of the publication processes, both print and electronic, and the policies, procedures, organization, and legal environment of their specific library or library organization.

Before you can assist library users to identify, locate, and access the information they need, you must know (in general and in specific subject areas):

- how information may be organized;
- how to identify and locate information;
- how to navigate, search, and otherwise delve into information-finding devices;
- how, where, and sometimes why information is recorded, stored, structured, and restructured through the publication processes (historically and in modern times, formal, scholarly, commercial, informal, official, etc.);
- how, where, and why information can be accessed and by whom, and under what conditions; and
- the costs, restrictions (memberships, subscriptions, licenses, security clearances), physical format, and condition of materials.

The reference competencies listed and discussed below are not intended to be a comprehensive list. As were the competencies discussed in the previous chapters, these are again a synthesis and consensus of those reported as critical by experienced virtual reference librarians and researchers. Each competency is described in terms of learning goals—the skills and knowledge to be learned—and performance objectives—what the learner needs to be able to do with what is learned. Each competency, along with any advanced aspects, is addressed with learning activities, advice and supporting tools for maintaining and building reference competencies. The learning activities and supporting tools are also available on the handbook's companion Web site.

Please keep in mind: Reference skills and knowledge must be understood within the context of a given library or library organization. Each virtual reference librarian will need to know or be able to do these things within the context of the library or library organization he/she is working for and with the virtual reference service users he/she will work with.

Interview Question 7

My worst ever reference interview was back when I was a GA at the UIUC Undergrad library. I was sure I knew everything there was to know about reference because I was very familiar with Dialog and our newly arrived CD-ROM databases, and when a student approached the reference desk wanting articles from journals from the turn of the century regarding educational philosophy/policy in the U.S. I was at a loss. I had spent very little time learning how to use Education Index or even Reader's Guide in print.

In your opinion/experience, to what extent does source knowledge in both print and electronic format important for chat reference librarians in order for them to work with the patron to develop a search strategy and deliver information the patron can use in a format they can use and require?

KP: Until everything is online (and none of us are holding our collective breath), information seekers will have to know what print resources are available and how to use them. I feel very fortunate that I was in college and grad school during transitional years—my college library had a card catalog and hard copies of *Reader's Guide to Literature;* my first and second grade schools had CD-ROMs to search for articles that then were hidden in bound journals in the stacks; by the time I finished my MLS, indexes were online and mostly full-text.

KnowItNow takes advantage of subject specialists during library hours. These librarians working in libraries with fabulous print collections have scanners connected to their VR work station, so they can take advantage of all their library's resources.

SM: Do you do library/information instruction or not? This tends to be a typical rift when librarians of different philosophies are all working together collaboratively on an online reference service. We need to think of "library instruction," "information literacy," and the like as a continuum rather than either you do this instruction full-on or not at all. Although we leave it to the discretion of the librarian to do instruction along the way, we courage staff to think of information instruction in a broader way. For example, within the chat environment, the librarian can "think out loud" through chat and/or tell the patron the process he/she is going through to find the information. This can be subtle and not extensive; or it can be very detailed. For example, the librarian can type, "Hmmm, for career research, I often like to start with the Occupational Outlook." Or, "We might be able to find this online, hang on while I check the online business database using 'knit fiber retail' to find a list in Colorado . . . etc."

Our staff report that they like doing chat reference because it is "real" reference. In other words, we get a lot more research reference questions online within an hour than we would on the phone or reference desk. Often "reference" questions in person or on the phone include a lot of directional (where is the bathroom), computer-related (how do I print), or library information questions (hours, policies, etc). However, online people have typically searched for information using Google and other search engines. When they cannot find something, they log in to AskColorado to "get help from an expert." Our questions include a wide range of topics (legal, homework, business), often with considerable detail (for example, how do I legally adopt my niece whose mother recently died in another state?), and require adept online searching skills. It is challenging reference.

━━━━━━━

PO: Source knowledge is especially important when you are working on a local info question. It is also critical in getting into the right ballpark without floundering and wasting everyone's time. It is important to know print as well as electronic sources since you want to give the patron a full answer, including not just what we can show right now, but also what he or she might like to pursue later. In addition, tact and a willingness to admit that you need to consult with a colleague will often save the day. Humility is an important quality for a reference librarian. No one knows everything. No library has everything.

In the online environment, there are many technical and intellectual-property barriers to sending everything that you would like to supply to the patron. Online databases have authentication issues, which can be very challenging. In Ohio, the public library KnowItNow service is statewide, so it is time-consuming sometimes to establish what the patron will be able to use with his/her library card. One saving grace: OPLIN has done a great job of working with authentications for a set of databases so the chat librarians can access them and actually push them to patrons without long explanations and log-in routines, which may or may not work, and which the patron may or may not have patience to navigate. This technical issue is important, and not always within the librarian's control.

━━━━━━━

JY: In email reference I think it is important to be extremely knowledgeable in source and search strategy, because you do not want your patron to wait and you need to answer the question within your reference shift while simultaneously working desk reference. Chat implies an instant answer, and even if you might have a bit more time with email reference, you still do not have the luxury of time to go bumbling around for information.

━━━━━━━

KLR: I think source knowledge is important, but I think having the awareness of the variety of resources available and that not everything available to you may be available to the person you are trying to help is key. If I have access to JSTOR, but the patron I am helping doesn't—it is possible that I'm not helping them, instead I'm frustrating them. Also it is very important in chat to be able to explain to the patron how to access things remotely, or to find instructions from their home institution that explains the process for the patron so that he or she can access things remotely. Once that hurdle is conquered, the focus can shift to resources and search-specifics. You have to be flexible to do chat service, just like you are on the general reference desk—you never know what kind of question you will get. I think that is the key to being successful at reference, whether chat or in-person, you have to be able to cope with variety—subject-specific source knowledge isn't enough—you must have a breadth of knowledge, or at least an idea where to look.

LB: What is more important (than source knowledge) is cooperation and knowing that if you can't answer a question, there is probably someone else out there with the needed expertise who can answer the question. Not getting down on yourself if you do not know something is important and in collaborative reference services, knowing when to refer a question to a subject specialist is important. This is what is so great about collaborative digital reference services.

JV: From the transcripts I've read, I think patrons who use chat to find print sources are not surprised to hear that their source is in print and they'll have to visit a library in person. I think most chat users have a pretty simple query that can usually be handled with online resources. If it requires more, usually people do not seem to be unhappy to be told to visit the library in person. Sometimes they seem to be using chat to verify that they need to visit in person, or perhaps to verify *which* is the best library to visit in person.

SH: In my case, my patrons are just able to use electronic formats, and among them there's no "in print list," "bibliographies," "atlases," etc. So, there is not a broad selection that we can choose among for different sources, and in consequence, it is not possible to instruct them in these kinds of materials. Of course, we replace the use of those materials, by using the Web (not always the best choice, but manageable).

Reference Skills and Knowledge for Virtual Reference Librarians:

- R1.1 Ability to be approachable—to maintain and project a welcoming and enthusiastic reference service attitude—through text-based communications
- R1.2 Demonstrate awareness of and ability to apply organizational policies relevant to any given user of a specific virtual reference service

- R1.3 Detailed functional knowledge of ready-reference sources of information, such as encyclopedias, almanacs, indices, bibliographies, and standard reference works in print and electronic formats
- R1.4 Demonstrate awareness of the best or core reference sources available in print and electronic formats, and of the range of information resources that may be used in the delivery of reference services for selected subjects and general reference
- R1.5 Ability to conduct good reference interviews, to analyze reference questions using knowledge of the structures, organization, and accessibility of information in print and electronic formats
- R1.6 Demonstrate awareness of the need to and ability to evaluate information resources for their appropriateness in level, scope, and format for a given user
- R1.7 Ability to develop effective and flexible search strategies including keyword and Boolean searching in library catalogs, licensed databases, and Web search engines (and know when to use advanced search options)
- R1.8 Demonstrate awareness of the scope and limitations of Web search engines
- R1.9 Ability to perform advanced searches in at least one major Web search engine (e.g., Google.com, Ask.com, Yahoo.com)
- R1.10 Demonstrate awareness of the scope and limitations of and the ability to use freely accessible Web reference tools (e.g., Wikipedia, IMDb, Crime Library)
- R1.11 Demonstrate awareness of the need and the ability to evaluate information quality of Web-published information, but also to think critically about all sources of information
- R1.12 Demonstrate awareness of the fee-based or licensed databases accessible to both the virtual reference librarian and any given user of virtual reference services
  - o R1.12.a Detailed functional knowledge of the fee-based or licensed databases accessible to both the virtual reference librarian and any given user of virtual reference services
- R1.13 Demonstrate awareness of how and where to search local holdings information for print and electronic resources
- R1.14 Demonstrate awareness of how and where to search the catalogs of other libraries and library organizations
- R1.15 Demonstrate awareness of and ability to apply the available options for appropriate information referrals

R1.1 Ability to be approachable—to maintain and project a welcoming and willing reference service attitude—through text-based communications

As discussed in Chapter 3, approachability in virtual reference service is threefold:

1. The virtual reference service access points must be where the user can find them and easily connect to the service.
2. The language used in materials and Web pages offering, marketing, and promoting the service must be jargon-free, welcoming and inviting.
3. Virtual reference librarians must use language that invites, encourages, and expresses their willingness and enthusiasm to work with the user.

Approachability is primarily a communications issue, but it is also an important aspect of reference competency. The approachability of reference librarians—whether they are welcoming and show willingness to assist users—is the single most important factor in whether information seekers make use of reference services or not. When information seekers were asked why they did not ask a reference librarian for research assistance they reported:

> . . . they were unhappy with previous service (42 percent), while 29 percent feared their question was too simple for a librarian and another 29 percent said they didn't want to bother the librarian.
> (Ross, Nilsen, and Dewdney, 2003: 44 citing Swope and Katzer, 1972)

User unhappiness (Ross, Nilsen, and Dewdney, 2003) has also been attributed to librarians not listening, taking over the question without involving the user in the question analysis and search strategy development, not being friendly, and similar problems.

It is a failure of reference service when we are not clearly communicating our willingness to answer or offer alternatives for answering users' questions. Sheldrick Ross (2003) named this "Negative Closure, or How to Make Users Go Away"; Ronan (2003a and 2003b), Hirko and Ross (2004), Mon and Janes (2004), and Meola and Stormont (2002) also address this failure of reference service. The following is an incomplete list of "Ways to Make Virtual Reference Users Disconnect and Never Visit Your Virtual Reference Service Again":

- With no explanation, or greeting, connect or refer the user somewhere else (other service, other agency, physical library instead).
- Ask the user why they didn't just use X reference book (or Wikipedia, or

Google, etc.), or why they didn't come into the physical library, or why they didn't just contact other service.

- After a quick Google, tell the user that there is no information on their specific subject.
- After a quick Google, try to convince the user to accept what was easily and quickly found instead of what they really want.
- Warn the user that the search is too expensive, too hard, too obscure, too time-consuming, or just too much trouble.
- Do a quick Google, push a Web page, and disconnect.
- Tell the user you are going to search X reference source but never come back to the chat or return the e-mail.

R1.2 Demonstrate awareness of and ability to apply organizational policies relevant to any given user of a specific virtual reference service

The policies and organizational details that all virtual reference librarians must be aware of are:

- Accessibility of licensed database options and policies
- Administration
- Average length of transactions/time limits/limit on number of transactions per user
- User satisfaction policies/evaluation of service
- Confidentiality/privacy policy
- Document or information delivery options and policies
- Eligibility for service (generally and for specific users)
- Follow-up options and polices
- Hours of availability
- How you will identify yourself to the user
- Inappropriate users/patron conduct/user behavior policies
- Referral options and policies
- Scope of service/limitations on types of questions/questionable questions
- Set-up of the service (context, locations, equipment available, connection requirements)
- Staffing
- Virtual collections/e-Libraries/knowledge bases/ or other information collections that support and supplement the virtual reference service

The list above is a synthesis of checklists and guidelines identified by virtual reference researchers (Hirko and Ross, 2004; Lipow, 2003; Ronan, 2003b; Meola and Stormont, 2002).

Learning Activity 4–1 makes use of an expanded version of the checklist for reviewing a given virtual reference service's policies. If you need to create a new policy or revise an existing policy for virtual reference service, Lipow's (2003) Chapters 5 and 6 overview policy essentials as well as good e-library collection and Web design features.

The learning activities are also available at http://www.kovacs.com/ns/chatrefbook/chatrefbook.html.

Learning Activity 4–1: Review Your Reference Service Policy

Use the following "Virtual Reference Services Policy Review Checklist" to review your own library or library organization's virtual reference service policy.
Virtual Reference Services Policy Review Checklist

1. Accessibility of licensed databases options and policies (See Learning Activity 4–4 below).
2. Administration—who manages, makes decisions on policies, schedules, and otherwise administers the virtual reference service?
3. Average length of transaction/time limits and/or limit of transactions per user—are there official limits or guidelines?
4. User satisfaction policies/evaluation of service—is the virtual reference service evaluated? How? Are users surveyed on their satisfaction with the service? How?
5. Confidentiality/privacy policy—Is there one? What does it involve? Are librarians allowed/required to identify themselves?
6. Document delivery options and policies—does your virtual reference service offer to fax articles, records, etc.? Will they e-mail attached files? Will they put resources on the Web for users to download?
7. Eligibility for service (generally)—who may use your virtual reference service? How is this eligibility guaranteed? e.g., login and password, library card number, zip code entry, etc.
8. Follow-up options and polices—are users asked to supply e-mail addresses for follow-up? Is phone service or in-person service available for follow-up?
9. Hours of availability—when is your virtual reference service available to users?
10. How will you identify yourself to the user?

11. Inappropriate users/patron conduct/user behavior policies—is there a policy for handling problems in virtual reference? Or guidelines?

12. Referral options and policies—are referral options available easily on the library Web site or otherwise accessible for the virtual reference librarian and user? Are librarians encouraged to offer follow-up, advising the user to return to the service if the referral does not work out?

13. Scope of service/limitations on types of questions/questionable questions— some libraries limit virtual reference service to questions identified as "ready-reference" or short answer. Does your library have this policy? How are these questions designed? How are librarians expected to clarify these limitations to users?

14. Setting up the service (context, location, equipment, connection require-ments)—what equipment, software, specific location etc. does an individual librarian need to have available and at what location must they be while they are staffing your virtual reference service from? e.g., Kent State/OhioLINK librarians just need a computer with their software installed on it, and e-mail access. The computer can be located anywhere.

15. Staffing—how many librarians are staffing the virtual reference service at any given time? Is it possible to refer to another virtual reference librarian? Is there backup for handling busy times?

16. Virtual collections/e-libraries/knowledge bases/information collections that support and supplement the virtual reference service—does the library maintain a Web-based e-library collection of ready-reference resources, tutorials, etc., for use by users and virtual reference librarians?

R1.3 Detailed functional knowledge of ready-reference sources of information, such as encyclopedias, almanacs, indices, bibliographies and standard reference works in print and electronic formats

Why an in-depth knowledge of print sources? Many live virtual reference patrons will come to you only after they have searched the Internet and found nothing. That means there's a good chance that what they're looking for isn't on the Internet, so you'll have to know print sources and how to find them as well as Internet sources. Of course you have to find them as well as Internet sources (Web sites and subscription database) too, because there's also a good chance the patron didn't find anything because they weren't searching correctly, or weren't searching in the right place . . .

(Meola and Stormont, 2002:118)

This competency is so basic that I almost decided to leave it out. Hopefully, it can be assumed that anyone graduating from an ALA-accredited library school will have this competency. Library school students and library paraprofessionals staffing virtual reference services may or may not have achieved it. In the virtual reference environment, it is critical that you know well the ready-reference tools you will always want and should be able to use, whether they are in print or electronic formats. The ready-reference tools—on the shelves near your work area or in an e-library collection—should be familiar to you.

The best strategy for developing detailed functional knowledge of ready-reference tools is to review them, book by book and Web site by Web site. Browse your library's print and e-library ready-reference collection. Familiarize yourself with the titles, locations, tables of contents, introductions, indexes, or search tools in each ready-reference source. Try to understand why a particular reference source has been selected as a ready-reference source by your reference colleagues.

The "Core Reference Sources and Tools" section below discusses some additional ideas.

Introduction to Reference Work, Volume I (Katz, 2002) may be useful for an introduction to the basic ready-reference tools. Tools such as *American Reference Books Annual* and ARBAonline—http://www.arbaonline.com/—will be useful for learning about ready-reference tools in more depth, as well as for learning about reference tools that are specialized for particular subjects and uses.

R1.4 Demonstrate awareness of the best or core reference sources available in print and electronic formats, and of the range of information resources that may be used in the delivery of reference services for selected subjects and general reference

The "Core Reference Sources and Tools" section below outlines some of the practical aspects of maintaining core collections—both print and electronic—of various types. At a physical desk, you can reach around and grab the best or core ready-reference sources from the shelves adjacent to the desk. You need to be able to do something analogous at the virtual reference desk. Core subject reference tool survey results are also reported below.

The Reference Collection: From the Shelf to the Web (Frost, 2006) provides a clear and current picture of both the state of reference sources in terms of their accessibility and their value, in print and electronic form, for reference service.

Gary Price's blog and newsletter The Resource Shelf—http://www.resourceshelf.com/—is the single most useful source for maintaining professional awareness of electronic reference tools, especially Web sources.

In thinking about what librarians continue to do better than electronic systems, I can't help feeling that the more things change, the more they stay the same. The difference is that the knowledge work corporate librarians performed in the mid–20th century involved fewer media types than it does today. And nowadays, more people with varied titles, are doing that work in many niches throughout organizations.

(Huwe, 2004: 39)

R1.5 Ability to conduct good reference interviews, to analyze reference questions using knowledge of the structures, organization, and accessibility of information in print and electronic formats (See also Chapter 3, Basic Communications Skills and Knowledge)

The best reference librarians know that they will need to elicit clarifying information from the user in order to select the best information sources to meet that user's information needs. Given the previous competency, reference librarians know what kinds of information sources will be available, and will ask clarifying questions of the user that will guide them in developing search strategies.

Learning Activity 4–2, after the next competency, offers some simple step-by-step models that can be used as a guide for most reference question analyses and search strategy development.

R1.6 Demonstrate awareness of the need to and ability to evaluate information resources for their appropriateness in level, scope, and format for a given user

An intermediate process between analyzing the question and developing a search strategy involves assessing the user's information need in terms of the educational level, purpose, form, etc. and then choosing sources for their appropriateness for the user's needs.

The reference interview should elicit specifics about the user's information need in terms of the educational level needed. If you are unsure, ask. "What kind of information do you need?" "Do you need research reports?" "Do you need summaries?" "Do you need something that you can use for your X grade homework report?" "Do you need something for your postgraduate research?"

Learning Activity 4–2 includes this aspect of analyzing reference questions and developing search strategies.

The learning activities are also available at http://www.kovacs.com/ns/ chatrefbook/chatrefbook.html.

Learning Activity 4–2: Analyzing Reference Questions and Developing Search Strategies

Connect to this Web-based workshop. You will be able to take the complete workshop self-paced via Web and e-mail with the instructor or merely browse through as you choose.

- "Beyond Boolean: Effective Web Reference Strategies"—http:// www.kovacs.com/bb/bb.html Login: chatrefbook Password: kovacs

R1.7 Ability to develop effective and flexible search strategies, including keyword and Boolean searching in library catalogs, licensed databases, and Web search engines (and know when to use advanced search options)

You need knowledge of search techniques because it's a basic reference skill, but also for the same reason you need knowledge of sources: virtual patrons will come to you after they have tried ineffectual searches or that have resulted in zero hits. Finding results quickly means knowing how to perform sophisticated keyword and subject search in a multiplicity of search tools.

(Meola and Stormont, 2002:119)

Once the question is analyzed and clarified, the first search step is to make a decision about potential sources of information. Is the best source of the information likely to be a book, a journal article, a statistical source, or another data source? A core resource might already be known to the librarian and would be the first choice. If that source is not successful, then consider another known source or select an appropriate reference source.

Good search skills involve knowing the basic features of search tools, including printed indexes, bibliographies, library catalogs, Web search engines, bibliographic databases, and full-text retrieval tools.

Keyword and Boolean searching is not necessarily the best first search strategy to use. In print indexes and bibliographies, a keyword or several optional/alternative keywords must be carefully selected in consultation with the user. Successful searching may be accomplished with a single keyword if that keyword is a name, title, or unique concept in most search tools. For more complex searching in online catalogs, Web search engines, and some databases, keywords combined with Boolean operators may be more effective. For full-text databases, they are almost always essential unless you are searching for a known item or very unique concept keyword.

Use Learning Activity 4–3 to find useful Web tutorials for learning keyword and Boolean search skills. It also links to some of the advanced searching guides Web search engines provide for us and advises looking for those guides made available by fee-based database publishers as well.

A virtual reference interview frequently includes giving good, clear, and usable instructions on how to search databases, as well as how to search, explore, and browse finding tools. Reference librarians need to know enough about searching to be able to give clear and accurate instructions.

The learning activities are also available at http://www.kovacs.com/ns/chatrefbook/chatrefbook.html.

Learning Activity 4–3: Web-based Tutorials for Keyword and Boolean Search Strategies

Visit one or more of this selected collection of links to Web tutorials for learning keyword and Boolean and other advanced searching options. Read, complete the tutorials, or otherwise make use of the learning resources to improve your basic and advanced search skills.

- "Invisible Web: What it is, Why it exists, How to find it, and Its inherent ambiguity"—http://www.lib.berkeley.edu/TeachingLib/Guides/Internet/InvisibleWeb.html.
- Guide to Effective Searching of the Internet—http://www.brightplanet.com/resources/details/searching.html
  Excellent, very detailed, discussion of how the Internet is most effectively searched, including advanced search skills in general. The Search engine itself locates specific databases as well as search tools.
- Google Advanced Search Tips—http://www.google.com/intl/en/help/refinesearch.html
- Search Better with Gary Price—http://about.ask.com/en/docs/about/garyprice.shtml
- Altavista Advanced Search Help—http://www.altavista.com/help/search/help_adv
- Search Engine Watch—http://www.searchenginewatch.com/
  The very best place to get facts and details about Web search engines.
- Search Engine Showdown—http://www.searchengineshowdown.com
- Learning about Searching—http://www.searchengineshowdown.com/strat/
- InfoPeople Project Search Tools—http://www.infopeople.org/search/
- NoodleTools—http://www.noodletools.com/
- "Choose the best engine for your purpose"—http://www.noodletools.com/

debbie/literacies/information/5locate/adviceengine.html
Designed for elementary school students to use in choosing a search engine.

R1.8 Demonstrate awareness of the scope and limitations of Web search engines

Simple but essential, this competency is easy to meet. Select one or two Web search engines and read their documentation. Read their search tutorials, their overview of services, their "About Us" information, and also find articles by others about those search tools. Greg Notess' blog Search Engine Showdown: The User's Guide to Web Searching—http://www.searchengineshowdown.com/—is a great tool to use maintain professional awareness of the latest Web search engine features. Search Engine Watch, http://searchenginewatch.com/, also publishes news and analysis of Web search engines.

R1.9 Ability to perform advanced searches in at least one major Web search engine (e.g., Google.com, Ask.com, Yahoo.com)

An Internet search engine can be your best friend, helping you to quickly clarify an unfamiliar topic or deliver information to the user... Knowing your guides to Internet resources and the library Web site is also key.

(Ronin, 2003a:46)

Choose one that you feel most comfortable with. Determine if it offers advanced search features such as Boolean and learn them. Go beyond the basic search instructions and study the advanced search instructions; these offer many features that are valuable for reference librarians. For example, you can use Google to search specific subject databases or everything in a given domain using their advanced search form or by typing "site:domain" (e.g., "site:medlinplus.gov") at the beginning of your search statement.

R1.10 Demonstrate awareness of the scope and limitations of and the ability to use freely accessible Web reference tools

Listed in the results of the core reference tools surveys discussed below are many excellent Web reference tools that are freely available. Some of these are U.S. tax-payer supported sites created and maintained by U.S. Federal and state agencies. Others are scholarly projects, supported by nonprofit foundations, universities, or volunteers, created and maintained mostly by volunteers. Still others are created and maintained by commercial entities and made "freely available" on the Web and funded by advertising.

IMDB.org, a site initially created by volunteers, and funded primarily by advertising, has been cited as an essential tool for many libraries for identifying movies, actors, and related facts. Wikipedia, a site created and maintained primarily by volunteers, and funded by donations and grants, has met with controversy. Some librarians use it frequently and view it as a best first place to get started on in-depth research—to get a clue where to begin. Other librarians feel that its open volunteer-edited nature automatically makes it a bad choice.

Berinstein (2006) in *Searcher* and Giles (2005) in the journal *Nature* have both evaluated Wikipedia in comparison to the classic *Encyclopaedia Britannica*. Giles used a scientific random selection of topic comparisons. Berinstein's evaluation was broader and included interviews with the editors and contributors involved in each project. Ultimately, the results are expressed in the title of Berinstein's article: " The Kid's All Right (and So's the Old Man)."

R1.11 Demonstrate awareness of the need and the ability to evaluate information quality of Web-published information, but also to think critically about all sources of information

The Web is at the same time a reference library, an archive of historical and literary achievement, a pile of comic books, and a stack of advertising flyers. The Web publishes academic, popular, specific, technical, recreational, inflammatory, biased, deliberately fraudulent, truthful, enlightening, proselytizing, documenting, and advertising communications, and more. The print publishing world is not so open, perhaps, but covers the same scope of human communications. Other media (film, television, radio, etc.) has a similar range of communications. Our media is the ultimate cultural artifact. Humans publish their diversity. Who we are, wherever we are, how we think, what we do, what we care about, what we find humorous, tragic, and more. All of this published information is potentially of interest to any given information seeker. One information seeker's treasure is another's garbage.

All librarians use the basic criteria for evaluating information every day. In evaluating Web information, it will be helpful to make those basic criteria explicit and to apply them consistently and rigorously. The real key is to know how to find the information that we need in order to successfully evaluate Web (and other) published information. The discussion that follows can be found in more detail and with learning activities for practicing in "Evaluating Internet Information," a free Web-based workshop at http://www.kovacs.com/eval.html.

Quality of information varies on the Internet because anyone can publish or communicate information on the Internet. In general, use the same criteria used to judge information from print or other media. Evaluation criteria for Internet information can be reduced to six questions:

1. Who provided the information?
2. What is their reputation as an information provider?
3. Do they have the authority or expertise to provide information on that topic?
4. What is the purpose for which the information is being provided?
5. Is the information provided for current information or historical purposes?
6. Does currency affect the quality of the information? And if so, when was the last update of the information?

Or simpler still, the underlying concept is reputation. What do you know and what have you learned to expect from a person or organization? Reputation is based on what we know about the authority and credibility of the information source and the purpose for which the information is provided.

In the United States, the general public has only had access to the Internet since around 1994. Reputation requires time and exposure to public opinion. Users can usually find out about the information provider and their authority, as well as about the purpose for which the information is provided and whether or not it is current. If you cannot at least find out who provided the information, however, then you cannot use it in a library, teaching, or research environment. All of us have been trained to cite a source when we answer a question. For example, my answers to the reference question "Who was Edmund Kemper and was he really a genius?" were:

1. According to Crime Library—http://www.crimelibrary.com/serial_killers/predators/kemper/edmund_1.html—Edmund Kemper is a serial killer known as the Co-Ed Butcher and, after murdering his paternal grandparents when he was 15, "He was sent for psychiatric testing and diagnosed as having paranoid schizophrenia. He was also found to have a near-genius IQ."
2. According to Wikipedia—http://en.wikipedia.org/wiki/Edmund_Kemper—Edmund Kemper is a serial killer, there are many details and links to published accounts of his crimes, and, "He allegedly possesses a near-genius IQ."

The information provider and authority information on Crime Library is given in "The Author" and "Bibliography" sections of the article about Edmund Kemper. The author's bio and other publications are listed. Attribution of Crime Library as a Web publication of the cable television program CourtTV is found on multiple parts of every Web page in the site.

In Wikipedia, there is no author of the Kemper article, but there is a list of links to supporting sites—including CrimeLibrary.com—and a bibliography. Clicking on "About Wikipedia" reveals the peer reviewing and volunteer contributor policy of Wikipedia.

Some Web sites do not provide such easy access to the information provider's identification information. To locate the information provider's identity, the first thing you need to do is read through the Web site. Most usable Web sites will provide an "About," "Who we are," or contact information in some manner. You may need to read through two or more pages, but it is necessary to read thoroughly and carefully through the site.

In order to establish the authority and credibility of an information provider, you should read through the site to find out the education, experience, research background, or other authority which the information provider says they have. There should be an e-mail address, Web form, or other contact information on a well-designed Web page. Lack of contact information may also indicate that no one is willing to take responsibility for the content of the Web page. If you think the information is important enough to do so, use your Web browser view source or view page option to look for possible author identification in a <Meta> tag field. For example, if you look at the "Page Source" for www.kovacs.com, you will see: <meta name="Author" content="Diane K. Kovacs

Some other strategies for establishing the Web site quality are:

- E-mail the person or organization apparently responsible for a site and ask them to answer the questions about information providers' education, experience, and research background.
- Ask a subject expert to review the information. Or, if you are a subject expert, use your own judgment.
- Find reviews of Web resources by qualified reviewers, or
- Use librarian created e-library collections to identify resources.

It can be very revealing to do a search of print directories or in fee-based Web databases to verify or validate the authority of an Internet information provider. You can search to see if they've published anything else in the area in print or other media, or you can search to verify any claimed professional qualifications. For example, most state medical boards now provide at least minimal licensing status information for physician's and some other healthcare providers. For example, AMA Physician Select State Medical Boards Web Sites—http://www.ama-assn.org/ama/pub/category/2645.html—or the Administrators in Medicine (AIM) Association of State Medical Board Executive Directors) DocFinder—http://www.docboard.org/docfinder.html—sites are good places to begin a search for physician credentials.

RI.12 Demonstrate awareness of the fee-based or licensed databases accessible to both the virtual reference librarian and any given user of virtual reference services

> In a setting where large numbers of databases are available, learning all of them may be problematic, but it is possible to master the searching basics of major proprietary search systems . . .
>
> (Ronin, 2003a:)

Inventory the licensed databases your library or library organization has access to and focus on those that the users have access to via the Web. Use Learning Activity 4–4 to guide you.

Detailed functional knowledge of the fee-based or licensed databases accessible to both the virtual reference librarian and any given user of virtual reference services

Information delivery is more than just being able to scan, fax, or transfer documents to users as discussed in Chapter 2. Virtual reference librarians must be aware of licensing and copyright issues related to each database the library or library organization has access to and the limitations on user access dictated by those licensing and copyright issues.

Some libraries include access details in their e-library collection annotations—for example, as a library user I use the Medina County District Library, which is part of the Clevnet library consortium. Clevnet uses the Cleveland Public Library's Databases and Links e-library collection—http://www.cpl.org/databases-links.asp—that identifies whether a given database is accessible to all library card holders in the state (OPLIN), in the consortium (Clevnet), or only for Cleveland Public Library (CPL) card holders. The list also identifies whether the database is available remotely through the Web or, if not, in which physical library locations it is accessible.

Check to see if your library or library organization already maintains such a listing. If not, you might want to develop your own list using the checklist in Learning Activity 4–4. Learning Activity 4–4 provides guidance on identifying databases and clarifying their accessibility through your library or library organization.

The learning activities are also available at http://www.kovacs.com/ns/chatrefbook/chatrefbook.html.

Learning Activity 4–4: Checklist: Database Accessibility

Make a list of the databases your library's users have access to through the library or library organization. Use the Database Accessibility Checklist below to review those databases to better understand information delivery and access issues for each one.

1. Make a list of the databases your library or library organization has access to. For each database answer the following questions:
2. Do users have access to this database through the library's Web site?
   - If yes, How?
     a. What is the address of the proxy server or other mechanism for access.
     b. Is a login and password required or library card number?
     c. How many users may access the database at the same time. e.g., one organization I've worked with has licensed the full-text NetLibrary database for their multi-campus libraries but only three students at a time may access it.
   - If no, Where and how will users access the database?
     a. In the library via the Web?
     b. In the library via CD or other local format?
3. Where are the search instructions?
   - Is there a link to search instructions on the library's reference Web page?
   - Are there links to locally created tutorials?
   - Are search instructions available in print or in a form that can be e-mailed?
4. Are users allowed to print records from the database? How often and what are the printing limitations—e.g., numbers of pages, numbers of records, etc.
5. Are users allowed to download or save records from the database?
6. Can files be saved to be e-mailed , faxed or saved to Flash/USB drives, CDs, DVDs, diskettes, or other electronic storage media? What are the limitations on saving records? number of records, file size or format?

R1.13 Demonstrate awareness of how and where to search local holdings information for print and electronic resources

Local holdings information includes where and how to access the library's catalog, e-library collections, as well as any print ready reference collection access. If you work for a consortial virtual reference service, you may need to be aware of the access to the consortial catalog or shared e-library collection, or to individual member library catalogs if there is no shared catalog.

Other related local holdings possibilities to be aware of are whether or not a scanner or fax machine is available for information delivery from print reference tools, or if a consortial knowledgebase or some other kind of shared answers to previously asked reference questions source is available for virtual reference librarians to use. For example, the Internet Public Library Ask a Reference Question service's FARQs (Frequently Asked Reference Questions)—http://www.ipl.org/div/farq/ or the University of Illinois Undergraduate Library's Question Board—http://web.library.uiuc.edu/ugl/qb/—archives.

R1.14 Demonstrate awareness of how and where to search the catalogs of other libraries and library organizations

A chat librarian needs to have a solid feel for online reference sources. I've found experience with my local catalog and bibliographic utilities such as WorldCat and RLIN are essential.

(Ronin, 2003a)

The Web-accessible union catalog Open WorldCat—http://www.oclc.org/worldcat/—and shared consortial catalogs such as OhioLINK—http://www.ohiolink.edu—and I-Share—http://i-share.carli.illinois.edu/—simplify achievement of this competency greatly. Identify any access to shared catalogs your library or library organizations has. LibDex, The Library Index—http://www.libdex.com/—is a directory of over 18,000 library catalogs. If you don't find one you think should be available, Google it.

R1.15 Demonstrate awareness of the available options for appropriate information referrals

In Chapter 3 we discussed the communications challenges of making referrals and doing user follow-up in virtual reference. The reference skills and knowledge aspect of this is to know the referral possibilities. Whom can you refer users to for additional information in any given subject area? For particular health, legal, business issues? The information you need to make appropriate referrals and user follow-up includes the kind of information that might depend on what kind of referral is to be made.

Many libraries maintain a list of local resources. If yours does, you should familiarize yourself with it. If not, make your own list of the resources that you think will be most important. Use a local phone book or interview your fellow reference librarians. A checklist of referral organizations might be organized by general referral type:

- Interlibrary referrals—special subject libraries or librarians
- Community referrals—health/government/legal/business/education
- Scholarly or research referrals—universities/colleges/institutes

Interview Question 8

Does your organization maintain a Web site or knowledgebase of some kind for chat reference librarians to use for frequently asked questions or to refer patrons to for specifics? Please share the URL if there is one.
KP: Wiki under construction for KnowItNow.

SM: We do not really have many frequently asked questions. Typically every day, the questions vary widely. The online resources also change so quickly that this type of knowledgebase might require more maintenance than the use would merit.

PO: I have not found the FAQ idea to be very useful. Knowledge grows every day. We serve our public best if we take time to search each question anew, starting perhaps with known sources. We want the freshest ideas, not canned. That being said, when we experience a class of students coming in over and over with the same topics in the space of a few days, we do "can" some Web pages to supply quickly to them.

JY: We cut and paste template answers for routine circulation questions (holds, renewals) and library policies, modifying the language to the situation (so they don't read like a response from a computer!). We have a template that we use for genealogists who believe they are communicating with Liverpool, England, not Liverpool, New York, USA. Every library response invites the patron to respond, make a suggestion or sign up for our email newsletter. I do not use templates for specific sources of information, although I do use a format called a click list that instructs the patron how to navigate "click by click" to find answers on our Web site."

KLR: No—we do have an operator survey, but that is more demographic data (what institution the patron is from; what institution the librarian is from; length of the question; subject area). Other than that, each librarian staffing the chat uses his or her own knowledge. We do have an online chat manual—http://

library.utoledo.edu/userhomes/wlee/chatmanual.html—but that is more about using the software and general policy.

LB: Being considered.

JV: Being considered.

SH: Yes, we have a Web site, but unfortunately the FAQ section has not been updated (how shameful!) but I constantly develop new guides and release news about changes in our collection, trying to keep our Web site up-to-date. *The URL:* http://bibliotecauv.tecvirtual.com.mx/ is in spanish, we are thinking of making an English version. but not yet.

Core Reference Sources and Tools

A well-organized, carefully selected reference collection is always desirable for providing good reference services. A good e-library reference collection enhances both the reference librarian's information source knowledge and the ability to access and deliver information for virtual reference service, as well as in-person users.

Some options for creating an e-library reference collection include:

Frequently Asked Questions Databases/Knowledge Bases
Bookmarks of Frequently Accessed Resources
Web-accessible e-Library Reference Collection

Kovacs and Robinson (2004) offer guidance and support for creating good Web-accessible e-library reference collections.

Once or twice per year for the past five years, I've been surveying reference librarians who participate in professional reference related e-mail discussion lists to learn what print, free or fee-based Web-accessible reference tools they consider most useful or even critical to performing good reference services. My "Core Reference Sources and Tools" site—http://www.kovacs.com/results/coreresults.html— reports the current results of my surveys of reference librarians, asking to identify the core print and electronic ready-reference tools that they find essential or they cannot work without.

References and Recommended Readings

American Board of Medical Specialties—http://www.abms.org. Requires registration; good privacy.

AMA Physician Select—http://webapps.ama-assn.org/doctorfinder/home.html?aps/amahg.htm.

AMA Physician Select State Medical Boards Web Sites—http://www.ama-assn.org/ama/pub/category/2645.html.

Administrators in Medicine (AIM) Association of State Medical Board Executive Directors) DocFinder—http://www.docboard.org/docfinder.html.

American Reference Books Annual. 2004. Westport, Conn.:Libraries Unlimited.

ARBAonline—http://www.arbaonline.com/.

Berinstein, Paula. 2006. "Wikipedia and Britannica: The Kid's All Right (and So's the Old Man)." *Searcher* 14 no. 3(March) http://www.infotoday.com/searcher/mar06/berinstein.shtml.

Cleveland Public Library's Databases and Links—http://www.cpl.org/databases-links.asp.

Core Reference Sources and Tools—http://www.kovacs.com/results/coreresults.html.

Crime Library—http://www.crimelibrary.com/.

Frost, W. J., ed. 2005. *The Reference Collection: From the Shelf to the Web.* New York: Haworth Press.

Giles, J. 2005. "Internet Encyclopaedias Go Head to Head." *Nature* 438 (December 15):900–901. http://www.nature.com/nature/journal/v438/n7070/full/438900a.html.

Hirko, Buff, and Mary B. Ross. 2004. *Virtual Reference Training: The Complete Guide to Providing Anytime Anywhere Answers.* Chicago: ALA Editions.

IMDb (The Internet Movie Database)—http://imdb.org.

I-Share—http://i-share.carli.illinois.edu/.

Internet Public Library Ask a Reference Question service's FARQs (Frequently Asked Reference Questions)—http://www.ipl.org/div/farq/.

Katz, William A. 2002. *Introduction to Reference Work, Volume I.* 8th ed. Columbus, Ohio: McGraw-Hill.

Kovacs, Diane K., and Kara L. Robinson. 2004. *The Kovacs Guide to Electronic Library Collection Development: Essential Core Subject Collections, Selection Criteria, and Guidelines.* New York: Neal-Schuman.

LibDex The Library Index—http://www.libdex.com/.

Lindbloom, Mary-Carol; Anna Yackle; Skip Burhans; Tom Peters; and Lori Bell. 2006. "Virtual Reference: A Reference Question is a Reference Question . . . Or is Virtual Reference a New Reality? New Career Opportunities for Librarians." *The Reference Librarian* 93:3–22.

Lipow, Anne G. 2003. *The Virtual Reference Librarian's Handbook.* New York: Neal-Schuman.

Meola, Marc, and Sam Stormont. 2002. *Starting and Operating Live Virtual Reference Services.* New York: Neal-Schuman.

Mon, Lorri, and Joseph W. Janes. 2004. "The Thank You Study: User Satisfaction with Digital Reference Service." 2003 OCLC/ALISE research grant report published electronically by OCLC Research. http://www.oclc.org/research/grants/reports/janes/jj2004.pdf.

Nofsinger, Mary M. 1999. "Training and Retraining Reference Professionals: Core Competencies for the 21st Century." *The Reference Librarian* 64:9–19.

OhioLINK—http://www.ohiolink.edu.

Open WorldCat—http://www.oclc.org/worldcat/.

Ronan, Jana S. 2003a. "The Reference Interview Online." *Reference & User Services Quarterly* 43 no. 1 (Fall):43–47.

Ronan, Jana S. 2003b. *Chat Reference: A Guide to Live Virtual Reference Services.* Westport, Conn.: Libraries Unlimited.

Search Engine Showdown: The User's Guide to Web Searching—Greg Notess' blog—http://www.searchengineshowdown.com.

Search Engine Watch—http://searchenginewatch.com/.

Ross, Catherine Sheldrick; Kirsti Nilsen; and Patricia Dewdney. 2002. *Conducting the Reference Interview: A How-To-Do-It Manual for Librarians.* New York: Neal-Schuman.

University of Illinois Undergraduate Library's Question Board—http://web.library.uiuc.edu/ugl/qb/.

Wikipedia—http://en.wikipedia.org/.

Index

About the Author

Diane K. Kovacs has more than thirteen years of experience as a Web teacher and consultant. She founded "Kovacs Consulting—Internet and Web Training" in 1993. Diane has designed and taught Web-based MLA CE courses since 2001. She also designs and teaches Web-based courses for UIUC GSLIS LEEP, the ACRL, and other organizations.

Her many books include: *The Internet Trainer's Guide* (1995) and *The Internet Trainer's Total Solution Guide* (1997), published by Van Nostrand Reinhold. With her husband, Michael Kovacs, she co-authored *Cybrarians Guide to Successful Internet Programs and Services*, published by Neal-Schuman in 1997. *How to Find Medical Information on the Internet: A Print and Online Tutorial for the Health Care Professional and Consumer* (2000) was published by Library Solutions Press. *Building Electronic Library Collections: The Essential Guide to Selection Criteria and Core Collections* (2000), *Genealogical Research on Web* (2002), and *The Kovacs Guide to Electronic Library Collection Development: Essential Core Subject Collections, Selection Criteria, and Guidelines* (2004), coauthored with Kara L. Robinson, were all published by Neal-Schuman

The Government Documents Roundtable of the American Library Association made Diane Kovacs the 2000 recipient of the "Documents to the People" award. She also received the Apple Corporation "Library's Internet Citizen Award" for 1992, and in 1996 became the first recipient of the Leadership Award from the University of Illinois Graduate School of Library and Information Science Alumni Association. From 1990 to 2002, she was the editor-in-chief of the Directory of Scholarly and Professional Electronic Conferences.

Diane received an M.S. in Library and Information Science from the University of Illinois in 1989 and an M.Ed. in Instructional Technology from Kent State University in 1993. She has a B.A. in Anthropology also from the University of Illinois, 1985.